LO

John Schofield

COLLINS
London and Glasgow

Picture Acknowledgements.
Diagrams and maps: David Ayres, Tracy Wellman. Original colour
artwork: Jim Renshaw, Metin Salim, Nick Shewring, all of The Garden
Studio. Reconstructions: Terry Ball, Peter Jackson, Alan Sorrell, Chris
Unwin. Original photography: Andrew Lawson. Other photographs:
Mary Evans Picture Library, Michael Holford Picture Library. Other
illustrations reproduced by permission of Museum of London (pp. 12,
14, 18, 20-1, 23-5, 28, 30, 32, 36, 37, 66, 81, 132, 211), City of London
Police (p. 17), and the Master and Fellows of Magdalen College,
Cambridge (p. 120).

First published 1987
10 9 8 7 6 5 4 3 2 1 0

Produced by The Paul Press Ltd
22 Bruton Street
London W1X 7DA

Designed by David Ayres

ISBN 0 00 459501 7

Colour origination by Reprocraft, London
Typesetting by Wordsmiths, London
Printed in Great Britain by Collins, Glasgow

CONTENTS

Introduction   4

The Coming of the Romans   10

Saxon and Viking London   24

The Norman Conquest   44

Medieval London   66

Tudor, Stuart and Renaissance London   112

The Great Fire and Sir Christopher Wren   132

Georgian London   150

Victorian London   164

Twentieth Century London   208

London's Museums   222

Index   235

INTRODUCTION

London is almost 2000 years old. Throughout the ages Romans, Saxons, Vikings, Normans, and many other peoples have made their mark here, constructing walls, bridges, roads and buildings to live in and to work in. This guide is about the remains they have left, and the way the past is celebrated and treasured in London.

London has expanded since its Roman foundation; although the remains of the Saxon and Viking period are scanty, traces of the medieval city can be seen in many places. The Tudor and Stuart city and the early modern capital of the British Empire can be revisited through their buildings and monuments. Here can be found the works of famous architects such as Inigo Jones, Christopher Wren and Robert Adam. Here also we can relive the times of Boadicea, Alfred the Great, William the Conqueror, William Shakespeare and Samuel Johnson.

The intention of this guide is to convey the history and character of London through the ages, especially through descriptions of buildings which are still extant; failing that, we have to imagine London in the more remote periods – particularly in the case of Roman and Saxon London – by using reconstructions and visiting museums (a list of which is given on pp. 222-235).

Throughout, the emphasis is on the tangible remains of London's heritage, embellished by some of the more colourful traditions and ceremonies. Most of the buildings described are in central London – that is, the City of London and Westminster. The most important, and accessible, of these are shown on the maps on pp. 6-9.

Why have these buildings survived? Many are royal or church buildings and have stood the test of time; others have been lucky. The remains described here have been subject to serious erosion by time, fire, decay, enemy action in war and the efforts of town planners to improve the city. Until recently old buildings were not honoured for being old; they were pulled down. Many are still under threat, and we must be constantly on our guard to save the Heritage of London.

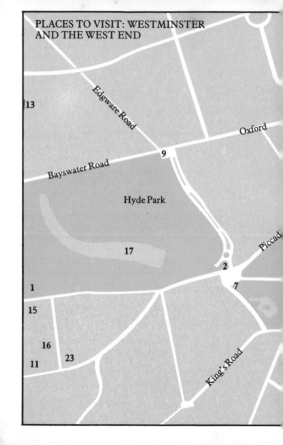

PLACES TO VISIT: WESTMINSTER
AND THE WEST END

13

Edgware Road

Oxford

9

Bayswater Road

Hyde Park

17

Piccad

2

1

7

15

16

11   23

King's Road

KEY
1 Albert Memorial
2 Apsley House
3 British Museum
4 Buckingham Palace
5 Horse Guards
6 Houses of Parliament
7 Hyde Park Corner
8 Lambeth Palace
9 Marble Arch
10 National Gallery
11 Natural History Museum
12 Nelson's Column
13 Paddington Station
14 Royal Academy
15 Royal Albert Hall
16 Science Museum
17 Serpentine
18 Somerset House
19 St James's Palace
20 St Martin-in-the-Fields
21 Tate Gallery
22 Trafalgar Square
23 Victoria & Albert Museum
24 Victoria Station
25 Westminster Bridge
26 York Water Gate

7

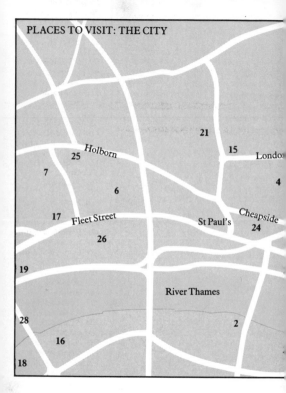

PLACES TO VISIT: THE CITY

21

15

London

Holborn

25

7

4

6

17

Fleet Street

St Paul's

Cheapside

26

24

19

River Thames

28

2

16

18

KEY
1 All Hallows Barking
2 Bear Gardens Museum
3 Cannon St Station
4 Guildhall
5 HMS Belfast
6 Johnson's House
7 Lincoln's Inn
8 Liverpool St Station
9 Lloyd's
10 London Bridge
11 London Bridge Station
12 Mansion House
13 Merchant Taylors' Hall
14 Monument
15 Museum of London
16 National Theatre
17 Royal Courts of Justice
18 Royal Festival Hall
19 Somerset House
20 Southwark Cathedral
21 St Bartholomew Smithfield
22 St Helen Bishopsgate
23 St Katherine's Dock
24 St Mary-le-Bow
25 Staple Inn
26 Temple
27 Tower Bridge
28 Waterloo Bridge

THE COMING OF THE ROMANS

INVASION AND REVOLT

The invading Romans crossed the River Thames in 43 AD. Exactly where it is not known, nor can we be sure what they found there. No certain traces of earlier settlement on the site of the future city of London have ever been found. If there was a settlement, it would have been a minor one. London is thus, effectively, the creation of the Romans.

Londinium was probably founded in the mid-50s AD, when the wave of conquest had already passed north and westward, and it had an administrative rather than a military purpose. The settlement developed quickly. Buildings and roads of a civil character were laid out over an ambitious area on two hills on the north bank of the river. The eastern hill is still called Cornhill, although time has smoothed out the contours,

Boudica or Boadicea can still be found in London – with her daughters in a chariot, outside the Houses of Parliament on the

Embankment. The 19th century sculptured group also shows clearly how each generation has its own view of the past.

and St Paul's now sits on the plateau of the western hill. Between them flowed a stream, later called the Walbrook, to empty into the Thames at what is now Cannon Street railway station.

Then, in 60 AD the growth of the city was temporarily halted. Boudica (Boadicea), Queen of the Iceni in East Anglia, rebelled against the harshness of the local military governor and led her tribesmen on a trail of devastation which only ended with London itself. The historian Tacitus tells of the massive evacuation of the unfortified city before the rebels' arrival, and the buildings of the period, when found, are generally bare. Some inhabitants remained to be butchered, hanged or crucified.

Roman reprisals were equally harsh, and the revolt was rapidly suppressed. The shock to the Roman economy, both in London and the rest of the province, was profound. Nevertheless, the Romans set about rebuilding with characteristic efficiency and within a few years had laid the basis for what was to become a major outpost of the Roman Empire.

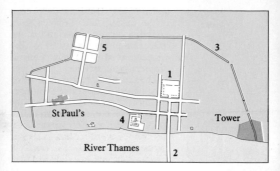

Above: *Roman London, showing the main features. Super-imposed upon the Roman city are modern St Paul's and the area of the Tower of London. The modern City of London is essentially the same as Londinium 2000 years ago.*

1 Forum
2 Bridge
3 City wall
4 Governor's palace
5 Cripplegate fort

ROMAN LONDON

By the opening of the 2nd century AD, Londinium was the undisputed capital of the provincial administration, with a population of about 30,000 Romans and native Britons, and with public buildings, monuments and public baths. The Thames was bridged as early as 70 AD, on the same alignment as London Bridge of medieval times; a corner of one pier was excavated at the foot of Fish Street Hill in 1981.

Below: Roman London in the 2nd century, viewed from the east. The forum and basilica dominated the town; beyond to the west lay the Cripplegate fort.

On both sides of the bridge the steep bank of the river was terraced with impressive buildings of locally produced Roman brick and timber. Below lay the quays which unloaded luxury goods for the new province and were the means of exporting its considerable wealth in natural resources. Behind the quays, on the higher ground around Cornhill, was a complex of buildings which formed the city's first forum: a basilica, serving as town hall and court of justice, with a courtyard surrounded by shops. Around 120, the forum was rebuilt on a larger scale to form the great square shown on the map (p. 12). The basilica was 167 metres long, the longest Roman building north of the Alps.

Most of the remains of the palace of the provincial governor still survive below the viaduct of Cannon Street station. Here, an official residence contained state rooms, a garden court with an ornamental pool and guest suites. The soldiers attached to the governor appear to have been housed in a fort built in the northwest part of town, known today as the Cripplegate fort.

Domestic buildings of the Roman city have been excavated on many sites; they were often destroyed by fire, and although occasionally luxuriously appointed, with mosaic floors and painted plaster walls, their construction materials were not particularly durable. Thus, apart from some mosaics (see p. 21), and the reconstructions in the Museum of London's Roman Gallery, it is not possible to see a Roman house in London today.

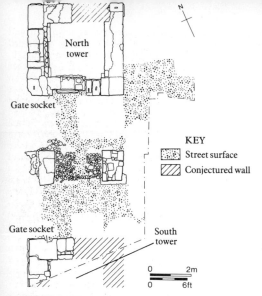

KEY

:::: Street surface

/// Conjectured wall

CRIPPLEGATE FORT

The Roman fort at Cripplegate was discovered beneath the blitzed cellars of the Barbican shortly after the war. The southwest corner was found first, on a site at Noble Street where the discoveries are still to be

Remains of the west gate of the Cripplegate fort, conserved below the London Wall. Parts of two gate turrets and the gateway between can still be seen.

The barrack buildings inside the Cripplegate fort; a reconstruction. This area is now sliced in two by the post-war London Wall carriageway.

seen. The corner of the fort swings away from the line of the city wall, which was actually built round the two outer sides of the fort a century later. The west gate of the fort is preserved beneath the modern carriageway of London Wall and may still be visited today. To the north and south of it, sections of the city wall are preserved in gardens; the section to the north includes three medieval interval towers, which were added over 1000 years later (see pp. 69-71).

THE CITY WALL

The character of the Roman city changed in the opening years of the 3rd century. Instead of the rapidly-growing port of the new province, it became the capital of the southern half of the province of Britannia and was transformed into a city of large buildings separated by open spaces, and surrounded by a formidable city wall. It had grandiose aspects which remind us today of such purpose-built capital cities as Washington and Brasilia.

The early 3rd-century city wall is over two miles long, and stretches in an arc from the later site of the Tower of London in the east to Blackfriars in the west, punctuated by five (later six) Roman gates. These gates were also used in the medieval period and have bequeathed their names to streets: from east to west Aldgate, Bishopsgate, Cripplegate (the north gate of the fort), Aldersgate, Newgate and Ludgate. The wall can still be seen at several points – notably Tower Hill, where the Roman work survives up to parapet level, as well as in the basements of several modern

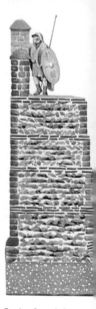

Section through the Roman defences of London, showing the construction of the wall and the bank behind. There would have been a ditch in front.

18

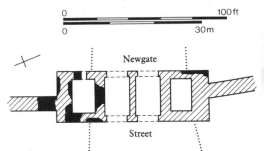

Reconstruction of the Roman Newgate. The plan shows which fragments have been found, some beneath the Old Bailey.

Newgate

Street

buildings. A pedestrian subway at Duke's Place, cut through the wall and its ditches in 1977, has a mural decoration showing the Roman defences at that spot. A special London Wall walk has been marked out along the line of the wall and gates between the Tower and the Museum of London, and visitors are often seen wandering with their map of Roman London through crowds of present-day city workers.

PLACES TO SEE

To the Romans, the town was an embodiment of the Mediterranean ideal of civilised living. A town would have as its focus a group of imposing public buildings such as the forum or market place and there would be public baths, perhaps a theatre or amphitheatre (the former semi-circular, the latter oval in shape), and several temples. Although several bath-houses have been excavated in London, little was known of other public structures until 1974-5, when a length of the

Reconstruction of the rites in the Temple of Mithras. The temple was probably built by a high-ranking civil servant as an extension to his own mansion in the Walbrook valley. The modern street running near the site is called Walbrook today.

A sculpture depicting four mother goddesses, later built into the riverside wall. One of the figures may be one of the Roman empresses of the 3rd century.

riverside city wall, of the late 3rd century, was uncovered south of Queen Victoria Street. In the fabric of the wall were sculptured stones from two monuments – a monumental arch and a free standing Screen of Gods. These monuments, pillaged for the later construction of the wall, must have stood nearby, perhaps in temple complex which may have lain south of St Paul's.

A few other fragments of the Roman city have survived. Mosaic pavements can be seen at the Bank of England and the church of All Hallows Barking, Byward Street. A fragment of a Roman building is to be seen in the crypt of St Bride's, Fleet Street (one of a very small number of extra-mural Roman buildings discovered); and the most famous archaeological discovery of Roman London, the Mithraeum or Temple of Mithras, can be inspected in Queen Victoria Street. Sadly it is not on its original site, which is about 50m to the west, and the restoration is not ideal. But it serves to remind Londoners of their long history, and has prompted the preservation and display of other fragments in modern buildings.

THE FALL OF ROME

The 4th century was the time of much unrest in the beleaguered and failing Roman Empire. In the middle of the century many town walls were strengthened with projecting towers or bastions, and London was no exception. A string of towers was built on the eastern half of the wall, facing the direction from which barbarian pirates and invading bands were to be expected. In the late 3rd century, the mile-long river frontage was also closed off with a high wall, perhaps also

Map of the Roman wall of London, showing the eastern and western series of bastions or interval towers and the gates.

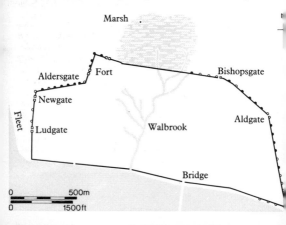

Reconstruction of the wall and an added bastion or interval tower in the mid-4th century. Outside the wall, the cemeteries are being cleared to improve the field of fire, and their monuments broken up for building the bastions.

with projecting towers. The 3rd-century quays, now in front of the defences, were partially dismantled and allowed to decay. Trade with the rest of the Roman world was badly disrupted. London, it seems, gradually wasted away.

The Romans left Britain, and London, in 410. In 457, the Britons are known to have fled there after a defeat by the Saxons at Crecganford (probably Crayford in Kent). After that, the city fades into the Dark Ages for 200 years.

SAXON AND VIKING LONDON

LONDON IN THE DARK AGES

Between the final departure of the Roman legions, when the lowland British were left to fend for themselves against foreign invaders and settlers, and 604, when St Paul's Cathedral was founded by one of the new local Saxon kings, there is little archaeological or historical evidence for London. We do not know how the city survived the 5th and 6th centuries, if it survived at all.

There is, however, no evidence for the old view of widespread destruction of Roman towns in Britain, and none at all in London. The riverside city wall and bastions show that the city was considered worth defending, but other evidence of the last years of Roman rule and what followed is hard to find. Within the walls, Roman buildings are generally covered by a thick stratum of 'dark earth', a deposit indicating decay and disuse, maybe

Silver penny minted in the reign of Alfred in the late 9th century, with a monogram of the letters of LONDINIA on one side.

Excavation in progress in Milk Street, north of Cheapside, in 1977. The mosaic of a 2nd-century Roman building was overlain by the mysterious 'dark earth' of the Saxon centuries.

even fields within the Roman walls.

By 604, when King Ethelbert of Kent founded St Paul's, London must have had a reasonable population. The new Christian missionaries, led by St Augustine, were shrewd men who would not have placed a church where there was no congregation. But we have no idea what the first St Paul's looked like; it has disappeared without record, replaced first by the medieval cathedral and then by Wren's St Paul's, which we know today.

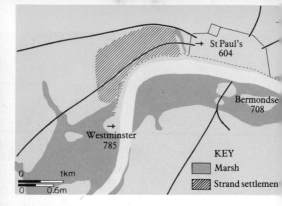

St Paul's
604

Bermondse
708

Westminster
785

KEY
Marsh
Strand settlemen

0   1km
0   0.6m

LUNDENWIC

In the City of London, over a
thousand years of redevelopment,
especially the digging of basements
beneath offices in the 19th century,
has removed many parts of the
ground where Saxon buildings
might have stood. The relics of this
early period are almost non-exist-
ent. It is not until the time of Alfred,
200 years later, that there are any
finds or structures on which we can
rely.

The Saxons built almost totally in
timber, and each generation of

ordinary buildings probably lasted for no longer than 30 years. How then could we expect them to last 1250 years? Their churches were often built in stone, but they have been rebuilt so many times that we have no idea what they looked like – except for fragmentary remains at St Bride's, Fleet Street, and All Hallows Barking, Byward Street.

We know that during the 7th and 8th centuries, London became a port and market – the Roman road system was intact, and the river was the main highway to the sea. In the 730s the Venerable Bede, writing his history in the far north at Jarrow, knew of London as a 'market of many nations, coming to it by land and sea'. But where precisely was this place referred to in contemporary documents as Lundenwic?

It was only in 1984 that archaeologists plotted all the finds of this Dark Age period on a modern map, and found that they concentrated around the Strand, just outside the City to the west. Here excavations have since found signs of habitation. It seems likely that here was a trading settlement, deliberately avoiding the old Roman city, maybe

27

because it enjoyed the security of royal protection and had no need of walls. Similar open, probably un-defended, sites have been excavated at Ipswich and Southampton. These places may only have been occupied sporadically at certain times of year, perhaps when foreign ships arrived.

THE VIKINGS AND ALFRED

The arch of re-used Roman tiles in the Saxon church of All Hallows Barking, Great Tower Street. This was only revealed through the destruction of wartime bombing. It may date from around 800 AD.

In 842 Viking pirates raided Canterbury, Rochester and London itself, causing many casualties. In 851, records the Anglo-Saxon Chronicle, 'three hundred and fifty ships came to the mouth of the Thames, and the crews landed and took Canterbury and London by storm'.

London's earliest Viking-period find dates to the time of these raids: 241 Saxon coins hidden near the river outside the west gate (on the site of the present Temple Gardens), dating to 841-2, and found in the last century.

Alfred became king of Wessex (southern England) in 871. He was obliged to buy peace with the invading Danes, who took winter quarters in London. For the next two years, until they were defeated in 878, they used the city as a military base. They were finally pushed out of London in 886. It seems likely that Alfred brought the population into the safety of the old Roman walls, and London became part of a network of fortified towns spread all over southern England.

STREETS, HOUSES AND WHARVES

Reorganisation of the old city must have followed. Judging from what happened elsewhere (e.g. at Winchester), Alfred, the church leaders and his successors contributed to the creation of a new city. Some new streets were laid out, mooring rights for boats and landing places were established. A dock in the Roman city is now known as Queenhithe, after Henry II's queen, but it was established by Alfred and named after his son-in-law, Ethel-

Reconstruction of an 11th-century house at Pudding Lane in the City of London from an excavation in 1981. Such houses are known in York and Dublin at around the same time. These are the types of homes that would have been lived in by the followers of Harold at Hastings in 1066.

red. The Roman bridge was probably rebuilt and re-opened.

We know some things – but not much – about the forms of ordinary buildings, the nature of the streets, and the quality of life. We can suggest that groups of timber buildings were gradually forming corners and frontages along major streets. These buildings were humble and low but often solidly built, and with thatched roofs. Shops, living accommodation and working areas were mixed together; there were craftsmen in bone objects, jewelry and leather. At the same time textiles from the Near East were being worn or used. Behind these buildings were pits containing industrial and domestic waste.

The best place to gain an impression of London at this time is not, however, in London but at the Jorvik Centre in York.

The relationship between Roman, Saxon and modern streets in the City. The modern Bow Lane was preceded by the Saxon street (middle) and, before that, by a Roman street (right). Saxon buildings are therefore to be found beneath the cellars along Bow Lane and other streets in the City.

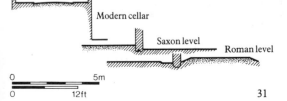

Bow Lane

Modern cellar

Saxon level

Roman level

0   5m
0   12ft

THE WATERFRONT

As well as Queenhithe, a landing-place at Billingsgate is mentioned in documents around 1000, about 100 years after Alfred's time. Excavations nearby have uncovered a bank of stones and timber, laid against the decayed Roman waterfront, as a form of hard standing on which the ships of the time would be drawn up. At one end, nearest the line of the old Roman bridge, a grid of stakes may have either protected the bridgehead against Viking invaders or, more likely, supported a jetty leading from the bank to the firmer shore behind.

Part of the waterfront area of London in the time of Alfred, from excavations in Lower Thames Street in 1974-8. A boat of the period is drawn up upon a hard standing of rubble and logs. Nearby, a grid of stakes may have supported a jetty.

LONDON BRIDGE IS FALLING DOWN

In 980 Viking fleets resumed their coastal raids. In 1013 Swein of Denmark attacked the city in earnest. At first the forces of King Ethelred – known to history as the Unready – resisted attack, no doubt aided by the desertion to their side of Thorkel the Tall, a notable Viking chief. But later in the year they submitted, and Ethelred fled to Flanders. After Swein's death in 1014 Ethelred joined forces with Olaf, king of Norway, and together they sailed to take London. *Olaf's Saga* tells how the Danes had made great fortifications around Southwark, digging large ditches, and building inside them walls of wood, stones and turf. Olaf covered his ships with hurdles against missiles from the bridge, and rowed up under it. There his men tied ropes round the supporting posts, and rowed their ships downstream as hard as they could. The posts were dragged from under the bridge and the Danish army, standing thickly on the bridge, fell into the river. The survivors fled into the city or into

33

Southwark. Thus Olaf and Ethelred recaptured London; and this may be the origin of the Norse song, and later English nursery rhyme, 'London Bridge is falling (or is broken) down.' Unfortunately, Ethelred died shortly afterwards and Swein's son, Cnut (or Canute), came in force and seized the crown.

Early in the 20th century, workmen excavating in the former foreshore of the river alongside the Saxon and medieval bridge line, found a group of weapons or tools which may well have been lost during one of the attacks on London Bridge.

ELEVENTH-CENTURY LONDON

No other military equipment of the Vikings has been found within the city itself, though other axes and swords have been found up and down the Thames. Some objects indicate a peaceful time through the 11th century, while Cnut ruled England (1016-1035). There is evidence of metalworking and producing objects from bone. Cnut is known to have been interested in chess, and bone chessmen, one with a projection in its base possibly for use in a travelling chess-set, indicate the Viking love of board games.

London's finest Viking monument also comes from the reign of

Viking battle-axes and spears have been found in the Thames near London Bridge – were they lost in Olaf's attack?

This Viking tomb-stone was found in St Paul's Churchyard in 1852. It marked the grave of a Viking buried about 1035. The inscription in runes along the edge reads 'Ginna and Toki had this stone laid'.

Cnut – a grave headstone, originally painted, marking the resting place of a Viking warrior buried in St Paul's churchyard, which was found in 1852. Along the edges, in Scandinavian runes, is the inscription 'Ginna and Toki had this stone laid' – but we do not know for whom.

At the same time, native sculptors continued to work in their own Saxon style; the cosmopolitan city absorbed the Vikings like any other new group, both before and since. This can be seen in the fragments of other grave monuments on display in the crypt of All Hallows Barking church, Byward Street.

THE NORMAN CONQUEST

After Cnut, English kings again took the throne; but the influence of the Norsemen, this time the Normans who had settled in what is now called Normandy, was growing once more. Their architecture preceded them; it was fashionable to build in the French style, and Edward the Confessor (1042-66) began an ambitious rebuilding of Westminster Abbey, next to his rural palace just upstream of the city of London. This church can be reconstructed from excavations and especially from its representation on the Bayeux Tapestry, that masterpiece of Norman war propaganda. On the tapestry, the Norman version of events leading up to the Battle of Hastings is shown; and among them is the death and burial of Edward, just as his church was being finished. Presumably there were several other such notable buildings, all churches, in the Romanesque style – St Paul's, for one, though we know nothing of its appearance at this time – since London was an international and increasingly cosmopolitan port.

London and Westminster on the eve of the Norman Conquest, showing the Palace of Edward the Confessor.
1 St Paul's
2 Abbey

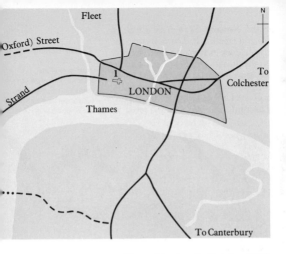

From this city, in October 1066, the new king Harold II and a rapidly collected army issued forth to meet another invader, Duke William of Normandy. One account suggests that they were so badly prepared that some of them took window-shutters from the city as shields. A few days later, the survivors of the ill-fated Battle of Hastings straggled back in disarray. In London they were at least safe for the time being,

39

as the Norman *Song of the Battle of Hastings* testified: 'London is a great city, richer in treasure than the rest of the kingdom. Protected on the left side by walls, on the right side by the river, it neither fears enemies nor dreads being taken by storm. The obdurate people conquered in

The Bayeux Tapestry shows the consecration of Westminster Abbey and the funeral of Edward the Confessor, whose death sparked off the

Norman Conquest.
This is the only
representation we
have of the Saxon
Abbey, a lost building
of European
importance.

battle sought this place, believing that in it they could dwell for a long time masterless..'

But William knew he had to have London in order to win the country. He took it by diplomacy and threat, and lost no time in clamping down on the inhabitants.

DI:REGIS:AD:ECCLESIAM
PETRI

THE
NORMAN
CONQUEST

ENTRY TO THE TRAITORS GATE

The White Tower still
dominates the Thames
at the seaward end of
the City of London.
Below the keep is the
entrance to Traitor's
Gate, a medieval
river entrance when
movement by river
was quicker and more
secure than by land.

NORMAN LONDON

By the time of the Norman invasion in 1066 the City of London was already 1000 years old. William the Conqueror, surveying the newly-won city in 1066, would have seen the old Roman city wall, still largely intact; some Roman streets, still being used; many Roman ruins, particularly the forum and basilica, probably then being pulled down piecemeal for their stones; and many smaller Saxon houses made of wood.

London was, by this time, the acknowledged capital of the kingdom, and William knew that he had to capture it in order to control England. This he did by persuasion and a little threat, and immediately set about controlling the defeated population. One of the first measures he adopted was to build three castles in the city. Two have disappeared; but the largest, the Tower of London, was to play a central role in some of the most dramatic episodes in English history, and remains the most enduring monument to the Norman Conquest in London.

THE WHITE TOWER

The original Tower of London, later called the White Tower, was built by William the Conqueror to overawe the 'vast and fierce populace' of London, who had submitted to him without a siege. It was, however, a fortified palace rather than a military fortress. Windows

Section through the White Tower, showing the strong foundations and the position of the king's Chapel of St John.

which are more than slits can still be seen on the third floor. Although the keep was a strong castle, with foundations 15 feet thick, it was designed to be lived in. The original entrance was the same as the present one, on the first floor. A spiral staircase then led to the floors above or the vaulted chambers beneath. On the second floor lay the normal suite of rooms for a great lord: a hall, a chamber and a chapel, here dedicated to St John. In the thickness of the wall a gallery ran round the hall one storey higher, communicating with the corner towers and garderobes (toilets). The name White Tower was first used after Henry III had it whitewashed inside and out in the 13th century. Its present appearance stems largely from restorations of about 1700

First two periods of growth of the Tower of London: left, in the time of William I and II (1066-1100); right, in the time of Richard I and John (1189-1216). Afterwards, the circuit of the castle broke through the line of the city wall and produced the concentric fortress known today.

when Sir Christopher Wren supervised the widening of most of the windows into their present shapes. The turret caps are Tudor, but replaced earlier, conical structures. In Tudor times the roofs also bristled with cannon, some trained on the unruly city.

The chapel of St John in the Tower is one of the finest untouched pieces of Norman architecture in the country. Its simple use of light, in an otherwise gloomy castle keep, is highly effective.

St John's Chapel

Within the White Tower, the room which has retained the most of its Norman character is the chapel of St John. The remarkable effects of the light here are due to the fact that the chapel protrudes from the southeast corner of the keep and has windows at two levels all round its curved apse. The cushion capitals, as shown here, were one of the most common features of the Romanesque style in England – a style of European architecture which the leaders of the Norman state and church brought with them. The Norman builders also re-introduced vaulted ceilings to an important space such as the nave of a church, as in this chapel, for the first time since the Romans left; not, as the Romans would have built them, in concrete, but in stone.

A bird's-eye view

This aerial view of the Tower today shows where the medieval parts can still be seen. With a bit of imagination, we can watch the fortress grow before our eyes. The core of the castle was the White Tower (**1**) (finished by 1097), originally contained within the southeast corner of the Roman city wall (the stretch along the river front, excavated in 1975-6, is preserved alongside the Tower's History Gallery). The keep was de-

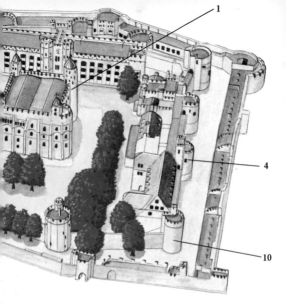

fended by a broad ditch to the north and west (2), which cut off the corner space. In the reigns of Richard I – the Lionheart – (1189-99) and John (1199-1216), the open space or bailey was extended to the west as a precaution against the deployment of siege engines and mining of castle walls. The lower part of the Bell Tower (**3**) remains from this time; it is polygonal, designed to present no blind spots and to deflect missiles. Remember that when it was built, the tower would have been lapped by the river. There were some unsuccessful efforts to make a wet moat around the new curtain wall. These developments, begun by William Longchamp, the unpopular representative of Richard I, were an attempt to make the king's principal fortress impregnable against the barons who supported John.

The succeeding kings, Henry III (1216-72) and Edward I (1272-1307), greatly expanded the rings of fortifications (**4**), breaking through the line of the city wall. Within the inner courtyard, Henry built a Great Hall (**5**); he lived in a suite of rooms which included the Wakefield Tower (**6**) where the Privy Chamber of the king can still be seen. Edward I also built two entrances: the Middle Tower (**7**) and Byward Tower (**8**) over the moat on the landward side, and an imposing river gate (perhaps modelled on that

The executioner's block and axe in the Tower of London. Only royalty or their close relations had the privilege of being executed on Tower Green. Many others met their deaths on the scaffold on Tower Hill, outside the castle.

at the French king's palace in Paris, the Louvre), which was later used as a discreet entrance for prisoners and became known as Traitors' Gate (**9**). Although part of the fortress, this riverside building contained state rooms and a chapel. Building accounts of the time tell of much stained glass, painted decoration and statues. Fragments of day-to-day medieval life in a castle can be seen as the visitor walks round: look out for the wall-painting of St Michael with the scales of divine justice in the Byward Tower, and, nearby, the winding gear for the portcullis, a great wheel with the lifting rope around its axle. In the Salt Tower (**10**) a 13th-century window and fireplace remain as examples of the style which many stone-built houses in London must have shared.

The Tower as a prison

The Tower has been used as a prison since shortly after the White Tower was finished. In 1100 Ranulf Flambard was able to escape by means of a rope, but the Welsh prince Gruffyd fell to his death when trying the same thing in 1244.

From 1322 those who plotted the downfall of the king (or who were accused, or suspected, of so doing) were regularly placed in the Tower. Vanquished kings and lords of enemy countries (in 1346, Scotland; in 1415, France) were 'lodged' here. Later, opponents of the monarchy were held in the Tower awaiting show trials which would dispose of them. Henry VIII especially used this method to rid himself of Thomas More and two of his wives: Anne Boleyn in 1536 and Catherine Howard in 1542.

The Tower had many advantages as a prison. Noble prisoners were usually tried in the palace at Westminster, and moved here by river (then the quickest method of transport in London). The Tower had plenty of space for solitary confinement in polite circumstances – its interval towers – and a noble or royal prisoner could have a suite of rooms, including exercise space on a parapet or flat roof.

Those condemned to death for treason were executed by beheading, usually on Tower Hill. A small number of prisoners, nearly all women, were beheaded on

One of the Yeoman Warders in the Tower. There are various theories as to the origin of their nickname, Beefeaters. Most likely, it comes from buffeteers, a French term used for the stewards of the king's buffet or side-table.

Tower Green, at a spot opposite the door of St Peter's church, to spare the government of the day the embarassment of a public execution.

Beefeaters and other traditions

The Tower has been many other things besides a palace, a fortress and a prison. From the 17th century it was an arsenal of guns, gunpowder and military stores. At the same time, surprisingly, many of the government's priceless paper records were kept here. The Tower also contained a menagerie. In the Middle Ages strange beasts such as a white bear or an elephant (a present from the French king in 1253) were kept here. The expansion of the empire in the 18th century brought lions, tigers and apes to make the Tower the largest zoo in Britain.

But the main traditions associated with the Tower are concerned with its central role as a royal fortress and prison. The warders of the Tower who had charge of the prisoners were called Yeomen of the Tower under Henry VIII. Today, they usually wear a blue uniform, granted to them by Queen Victoria in 1858, but they are better known in their dress uniform of scarlet and gold, dating from 1552. The Tower also still has a garrison of soldiers who take part in the 700-year old Ceremony of the Keys every night at seven minutes to ten, and whose responsibility it is to guard the Crown Jewels.

Some famous prisoners

Of all the stories which are associated with the Tower, three have a place in English folklore: the death of George, Duke of Clarence, the fate of the Princes in the Tower, and the pitiful story of England's queen for nine days, Jane Grey.

It is a popular legend that Clarence died in a butt (barrel) of malmsey wine. But did he? Clarence was part of an attempt by the nobles to stage a coup against the new king Edward IV in 1470, by bringing back the sick Henry VI from imprisonment in the Tower. Within days Henry was found dead in the oratory of the Wakefield Tower. Clarence, the King's brother, was forgiven, but he continued plotting and was thrown into the Tower in 1478. He was condemned to death

Several rooms in the Tower have now been furnished to show how the famous prisoners may have spent their time. The appearance of a room in a medieval castle is, however, best given by this room in the Salt Tower, with its early fireplace – a considerable luxury at this time. The window may also have been glazed, a luxury hardly heard of in ordinary houses.

and executed. There are various theories about how the legend arose: his body may have been removed from the Tower in a barrel, or he may actually have demanded this form of execution.

Five years later occurred the affair of the Princes in the Tower. Edward IV had died, and his son Edward V was only 12 years old. His claim to the throne was contested by his uncle, Richard, Duke of Gloucester. Both stayed in the Tower as Richard, officially the king's Protector, plotted Edward's downfall. He brought the king's nine-year-old brother, Richard of York, to the Tower; then announced that both princes had been born bastards. The implication was that the throne should pass to Edward IV's brother – himself. The princes were never seen again.

In 1674 a chest containing the skeletons of two children was discovered beneath the staircase leading to the White Tower. Most historians accept that these were the bodies of the princes. But the crime itself is still shrouded in mystery, complicated by the mixing together of popular myth and the great campaign of propaganda associated with the Tudor dynasty which overthrew Richard.

These two incidents have left no physical traces in the Tower; but the third story has. When Edward VI was dying in 1553 he instructed that the crown should pass to his cousin, Lady Jane Grey; she was proclaimed Queen at the Tower. Edward's

Portrait of Lady Jane Grey, England's Queen for nine days, beheaded in 1554, She was one of many victims of 'Bloody Mary', elder sister of Elizabeth I, who reigned from 1553 to 1558.

sister Mary rallied her own supporters and within a week had taken control. Jane and her new young husband, Guildford Dudley, were placed under guard in separate rooms in the Tower. In the Beauchamp Tower, so legend has it, Dudley carved his wife's name on the walls. At first Mary hoped to spare the couple but a further popular uprising made it too dangerous. Dudley was executed on Tower Hill and Jane Grey, having seen his body return, was beheaded on Tower Green.

THE MONASTERIES

Besides the Tower, the Normans built two smaller castles at the west end of the City, but their sites have long been built over. London was also enriched with a number of monasteries and hospitals, many of which were founded in the two centuries following the Norman invasion. They were large scale developments, often built of stone and rich in decoration. When civic leaders thought about any improvements to the city, they were probably influenced by the high standards of construction, plumbing and drainage in the new religious precincts.

There are two relics of the early medieval monasteries in London which can be visited today: St Bartholomew's Priory, and the Temple church, south of Fleet Street. St Bartholomew's in Smithfield was half demolished at the Reformation; the present churchyard is on the site of the long monastic nave. This is why the scale of the remaining church, formerly only the chancel (in other words, less than half the monastic church)

Plan of St Bartholomew's Priory, Smithfield, begun in 1123. The nave was torn down at the Reformation in the 16th century, and is now a graveyard. The choir of the monastic church remains as a startling, out-of-scale building. The cloister of this Augustinian Priory lay to the south, with the Chapter House, dormitory and other buildings (now built over). London was ringed with many such large churches by 1200.

1 Ladychapel
2 Chapter house
3 Prior's house

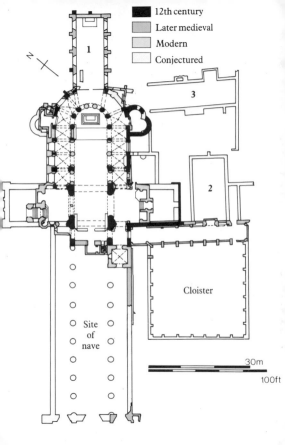

12th century
Later medieval
Modern
Conjectured

N

1

3

2

Cloister

Site
of
nave

30m
100ft

A detail of the choir of St Bartholomew's, showing the early 16th-century oriel window inserted by the last prior, Prior Bolton. On the window is carved his rebus – a bolt and a tun (barrel), as a reminder of his building. From the room behind the window, the prior could watch the Mass without joining his brethren.

Right: three capitals from the Temple Church, of the late 12th century. A certain variety was allowed in stone-carving, although not in later styles.

is so impressive. Here, built a generation or so after St John's chapel in the Tower, the arches are recessed in two rings or orders and a billet moulding follows the arch. In the triforium above appears the cushion capital, another Romanesque trade-mark. Although now a fragment, the church would originally have been of cathedral size; its nearest analogy is Norwich Cathedral. London would have had several of these large churches, each within its own high-walled precinct, within the city boundaries.

The Temple church, part of the religious house of the Knights Templar, shows the development of architecture in stone over the succeeding century. It comprises two main parts: a circular nave of 1185 and a 13th-century Gothic extension to the east. The west doorway, originally the entrance into the church from the cloister, is a fine (though much restored) example of a Norman doorway; here the luxurious carving derives from the Crusade-inspired fashion for eastern carving and design. Within the nave, the heavy round arches of early Norman times have given way

61

The circular nave of the Temple Church, consecrated in 1185. The shafts of the columns are in dark Purbeck marble. Set into the floor are 13th-century effigies of knights.

to graceful pointed arches and columns of Purbeck marble. Set into the floor are 13th-century effigies of knights, also of Purbeck. To the east the 13th-century chancel is a small-scale reminder of the interior of Westminster Abbey, then also being built a couple of miles away.

THE MEDIEVAL CITY

It is no wonder then, with all this building, that early representations of London show it as a forest of towers and spires. By 1200, most of the 107 parish churches which thronged London's streets are known in documents. Whenever a church site is excavated archaeologically before modern development, foundations from the Norman (and occasionally Saxon) period are found. The street pattern was a mixture of the Roman grid and Saxon amendments, short-cuts and developments. In the medieval period which followed, the city was to expand physically into the river along the mile-long waterfront, and to begin pushing out its suburbs

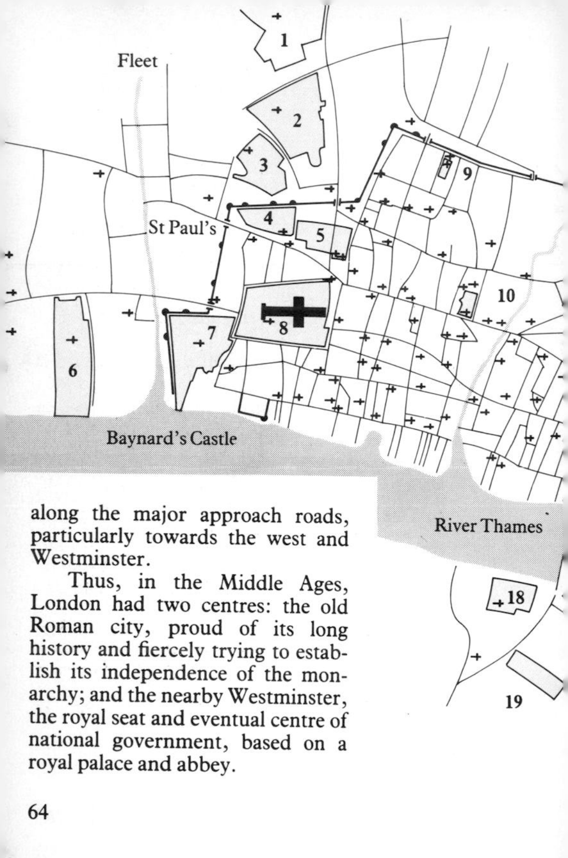

Fleet

1

2

3

St Paul's

4

5

9

8

7

6

10

Baynard's Castle

along the major approach roads, particularly towards the west and Westminster.

Thus, in the Middle Ages, London had two centres: the old Roman city, proud of its long history and fiercely trying to establish its independence of the monarchy; and the nearby Westminster, the royal seat and eventual centre of national government, based on a royal palace and abbey.

River Thames

18

19

Map of medieval London, showing the 107 parish churches, and the main religious houses:

1 Charterhouse
2 St Bartholomew's Priory
3 St Bartholomew's Hospital
4 Greyfriars (Franciscans)
5 St Martin-le-Grand
6 Whitefriars (Carmelites)
7 Blackfriars (Dominicans)
8 St Paul's Cathedral
9 Elsing Spital (blind hospital)
10 St Thomas of Acon hospital
11 Austin Friars
12 St Anthony's hospital
13 St Mary Bethlem (insane hospital)
14 St Helen's Priory
15 Holy Trinity Priory
16 Crutched Friars
17 Minoresses
18 St Mary Overey Priory
19 St Thomas's Hospital
20 St Mary Spital

Many of these names are still to be found in the streets or areas of the present City of London.

MEDIEVAL LONDON

By 1200 London was certainly the largest city in Britain and was matched for size only by such cities as Venice, Rome, Paris or Bruges. By this time also the kings of England, who normally travelled around their kingdom – so that the capital was where the king happened to be – settled at Westminster, and the organs of government gradually became fixed in the streets around the king's palace near the Abbey.

The City comprised 330 acres within its wall, and knights and bishops wishing to attend the king at court flocked to the capital, bringing with them wealth from the provinces. London drew sustenance from the country and prospered.

LONDON BRIDGE

The London Bridge which was to last, with many rebuildings, until

Above: the early 13th-century Common Seal of the City of London, showing St Paul guarding his city. It is inscribed, in Latin, 'Seal of the Barons of London'.
Right: a medieval joust on London Bridge. In 1390, Sir David de Lindsay, a Scottish knight, quarrelled with Lord Welles, the English ambassador to Scotland. Honour was satisfied by a joust in the presence of Richard II and his court. Lord Welles was unseated and injured, but the chivalrous de Lindsay ran to his aid.

1831, was built in 1176–1209. It had 19 arches and a drawbridge. Heads of executed traitors and criminals were displayed on the Bridge Gate, as shown by Wyngaerde in a drawing of about 1540. Recent work has dismissed the idea that the Saxons had a separate bridge downstream of the medieval one; it seems now that the Roman, Saxon and medieval bridges were all built on the same alignments.

On the bridge, there was a chapel dedicated to the city's adopted saint, Thomas Becket, and other houses soon followed. Throughout the middle ages, the southern approach to the city of London was through this strange tightly-packed street, like the Ponte Vecchio in Florence. Besides being an arterial road, it was also used for joustings.

ST PAUL'S

Old St Paul's perished in the Great Fire of 1666, but small parts of the foundations must lie buried safely (apart from the action of tree roots) in the Churchyard around Wren's cathedral. This is because the present cathedral was built on a slightly different alignment to its predecessor. Thus the foundations of part of the medieval cloister on the south side can still be inspected. We can stand by the statue of Queen Anne in front of the present west

Medieval St Paul's from the south. This Victorian drawing shows the details added by Inigo Jones in the 1630s, but also the spire which had burned down in 1561. Always look carefully at reconstructions!

The statue of a Black Friar over the door of the pub of that name in Queen Victoria Street, EC3. The pub is over part of the priory, near the riverside.

end and be above the west end of the pre-Fire cathedral, which was longer than its successor. Longer than Winchester Cathedral, with a tower and spire higher than those of Salisbury Cathedral, medieval St Paul's would have dominated the skyline of the city when viewed from every direction.

THE CITY WALL AND THE FRIARIES

The Roman wall of the early 3rd century largely contained the medieval city until the 16th century, but there were exceptions. The development, during the 12th century, of suburbs along the approach roads (especially along the Strand, between the City and Westminster) was one; and a small-scale expansions of the walled area in the southwest corner, caused by the arrival of the Blackfriars in 1275, was another. The Tower also pushed eastwards through the city wall during one of its periods of expansion.

The city wall, stretching from north of the Tower moat round to

Blackfriars, was 2 miles 208 feet long. Medieval repairs to the old Roman wall can be seen on the special wall-walk at Tower Hill, Cooper's Row and St Alphege's Churchyard at London Wall. At Cooper's Row a length 110 feet long includes round-headed openings, probably embrasures, and traces of a stair to the walkway. In the section in St Alphege's churchyard can be seen the brick parapet added in a rebuilding of 1477, when low brick arches were also added to the rear of several sections of the wall, perhaps as a defence against cannon.

Reconstructed foundation of bastion 11A, discovered in the blitzed cellars of the Barbican in 1965. It was one of several towers added to the city wall in medieval times. In the next tower along the wall lived a hermit.

As in other medieval towns, the various groups of Friars tended to build their religious establishments just inside the city walls, where land was cheap and comparatively undeveloped. The Greyfriars established themselves near Newgate Street in 1239, and the Blackfriars in the area around the present Blackfriars station and bridge in 1275; the city wall was rebuilt to go round their precinct. The Whitefriars chose to live in the suburbs, south of Fleet Street, where they expanded their property by reclaiming ground from the river.

The Friars' churches were specially designed for preaching, and they had a profound effect on the design of parish churches, not only in London but in the country as a whole.

CITY MANSIONS

From the 10th century London had been international port, and from the 11th century Westminster had become the seat of kings, where henceforward the monarch would be crowned. By the time of the Norman Conquest London was already the biggest city in the

A view of the back of the town house or Inn of the Bishop of Ely in Holborn. A hall (left) leads to a private quadrangle or cloister (centre) and the private chapel (right).

View of the Palace of the Bishop of Ely in Holborn London, Taken 1776 ...

The chapel has survived as St Ethel-dreda's, Ely Place. Such two-floored chapels are known in royal palaces, e.g. Saint Chapelle in Paris.

country. These three circumstances combined to make London the centre of England's import and export trade, and of its religious and political affairs. Thus the many nobles, knights, religious leaders and civil servants who formed the

for it was pulled down = At present on its vertue is built a Street called Ely Place wide of the Cloister to y left the great Hall, before y end is seen part of Hatcham, above part of

royal court or its bureaucracy needed town houses in London. We know of scores of these houses from documents, but little physical evidence has survived. The fragments that remain are from the houses of the Bishop of Winchester in Southwark and the Bishop of Ely in Holborn.

Both archbishops, 18 bishops, at least 22 abbots and at least six priors established town houses in London or its suburbs during the middle ages. There were two purposes for such a house. The first was to provide accommodation for those

engaged in everyday affairs, such as the selling of produce or the buying of goods. The second was to function as the town house of the institution's head when in London, especially when in attendance on the king at Westminster. First to settle in the Strand area, by 1225, was probably Ralph Neville, Bishop of Chichester; by 1253 five other bishops and the Archbishop of York had houses in the area. The Archbishop of Canterbury had already settled in Lambeth in the last decade of the 12th century.

Though detailed information is largely lacking, it is fair to assume that these mansions were comparable in size and architecture to royal houses. The Bishop of Ely's house in Holborn, built late in the sequence around 1290, included a private chapel on two floors which should be compared with royal chapels such as St Stephen's Chapel within Westminster Palace (see pp. 110-11) – with which it may have shared the same architect, Michael of Canterbury – and Saint Chapelle in the French royal palace in Paris. It survives today as St Etheldreda's, Ely Place.

The main styles of medieval window-forms between about 1220 and 1450. The date of construction of a building can be suggested by a study of the doors, windows and other details.

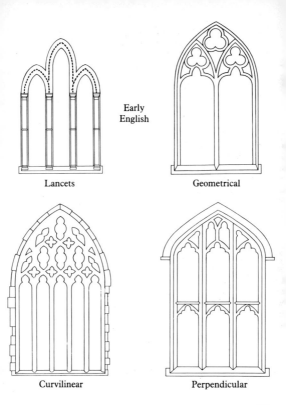

Early
English

Lancets

Geometrical

Curvilinear

Perpendicular

77

THE ARMS OF THE CITY

The square mile of the City of London still retains some of its medieval privileges, protected by successive royal charters, and symbolised by the City's coat of arms. This shows a shield with the cross of St George, patron saint of England: the sword represents St Paul, guardian saint of the city. The two lions are derived from the mayor's seal while the dragons are probably a badge of the Tudors.

The arms of the City of London. The privileges and wealth of the medieval city were assured by successive royal charters, reaching their peak in the 14th and 15th centuries.

DICK WHITTINGTON

London had a mayor in the last years of the 12th century. Along with other major European cities, London developed a town council, which organised the city's markets, formulated building regulations to improve construction standards, drainage and fire prevention, and to solve trade disputes and dispense justice. The concept of town planning hardly existed and rules had to be developed by experience. Walls three feet thick were demanded as fire-breaks, and better building techniques were demanded for cesspits of privies to stop foul leakages. The mayor was the figure-head of this accumulated wisdom which relied on custom – or normal practice – as much as on written regulations. The mayor was usually a rich citizen (he had to be to survive the term of office) from one of the more prominent trades. The most famous mayor was of course Richard (Dick) Whittington.

Whittington was a well-off merchant who traded in the risky but profitable North and Mediterranean seas; he sold silks and other luxuries

The real Dick Whittington, a merchant who made his fortune from trading in the risky North and Mediterranean Seas.

to the royal household. He also helped finance the campaigns of Henry V which included the battle of Agincourt. At his death in 1423 he bequeathed his considerable fortune to many charitable enterprises, among them a library at Guildhall (one of the earliest in Europe), almshouses and large donations to hospitals. Many London merchants were doing the same on a smaller scale: their wealth was put back into the city in the form of rebuilt gates, churches, repaved roads and other civic improvements.

London's insistence on self-government, once often regarded with fear and mistrust by the sovereign, is symbolised by ceremonials attached to the office of Lord Mayor. On the second Saturday of November every year, the Lord Mayor's Show is held in the City. The Lord Mayor is carried in his State Coach, built in 1757, drawn by six horses. At the Royal Courts of Justice in the Strand the mayor must swear an oath of loyalty to the monarch in front of the Lord Chief Justice. This custom dates from 1215 when King John granted

The Lord Mayor's coach is seen every November, carrying the new incumbent at the Lord Mayor's Show. For the remainder of the year, this gilded coach is kept at the Museum of London.

the citizens the right to elect their own civic leader. Thus when the mayor was elected he and many city dignitaries went to meet the king at Westminster. In the Middle Ages the journey was normally made by barge up the Thames, for the wide river allowed much more pageantry and show than the roads. The entire journey was made by road after 1857. Today, the Lord Mayor's Show is the nearest London has to a Carnival, with many colourful floats representing the City's past, present, and even its future.

GUILDHALL

The centre of government of the City of London is Guildhall, north of Gresham Street. Guildhall has stood on part of its present site from at least just before the end of the 14th century, and possibly from about 1130. It is likely that a Guildhall in stone was built or

Reconstruction of the medieval Guildhall around 1500. The porch was adorned with figures of Justice, Law and other civic virtues.

rebuilt in 1270-90, the probable date of the surviving western undercroft.

In 1411 John Croxton was engaged by the City to rebuild the Guildhall, less than a decade after the completion of the king's Westminster Hall. He chose to extend the building to the east with a new undercroft, which is the one visitors normally see. Above, the hall and its original porch, refaced in the 18th century, have survived both the Great Fire and the Blitz. Look out for the original 15th century window-seat and window fittings on the south side. The blank arcading on the insides of the porch walls was repeated in screens of tracery along the higher parts of the walls of the main hall, to give an effect like the interior of a cathedral.

83

COMPANIES AND GUILDS

Only four or five companies are known to have possessed halls before 1400: the Goldsmiths (1339), Merchant Tailors (1347), possibly the Skinners (probably 1380, certainly by 1408), Cordwainers (1393) and Saddlers (shortly before 1400). Of these, only Merchant Taylors' Hall survives. A large mansion with gates to Cornhill and Threadneedle Street (then called Broad Street) passed in 1347 from John Yakesley, tent-maker to the king, to a group of his fellow merchant tailors and linen-drapers. The existing hall can be dated only roughly to the 14th century, and thus it is not clear whether Yakesley or the company built it; two surviving bays of an undercroft, which extended at least one further bay to the north, at the east end of the building, may well be a relic of the private house and precede the walls of the hall. The medieval kitchen, on its present site by 1388 and rebuilt in 1432-3, could also incorporate fragments of the previous mansion. By 1600, there were at least 46 such halls dotted throughout the City.

Merchant Taylor's Hall, Threadneedle Street: a medieval livery company hall. The 14th-century hall and kitchen may be relics of a medieval mansion which became the craft hall of the tailors who, like several other companies, grew rich on their royal connections.

1 Hall
2 Undercroft
3 Kitchen
4 Garden
5 Parlour

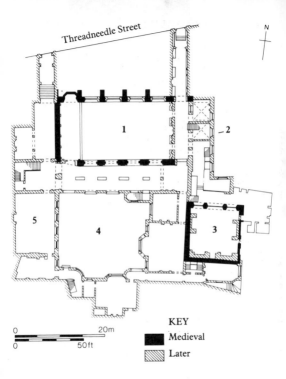

Threadneedle Street

N

1

2

3

4

5

KEY

■ Medieval

▨ Later

0   20m

0   50ft

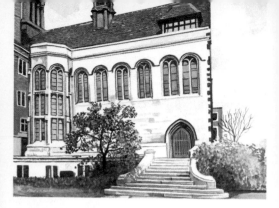

CROSBY PLACE

Crosby Hall, part of the house of John Crosby, a grocer and member of parliament who was knighted for his services to Edward IV, can still be seen at Chelsea (where it was removed in 1907). It illustrates the narrow gap between the house of a wealthy merchant and the palace of a real monarch.

Crosby originally built the house in Bishopsgate, in 1466-75, on the site of an already large mansion, which had once been occupied by a distinguished Italian merchant. He

Crosby Hall as it is today, on the site in Chelsea to which it was moved in 1907. Though far from its original site in the City, it is our best relic of the palatial mansions built by wealthy City merchants.

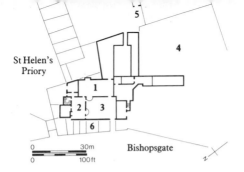

Plan of the original site of Crosby Hall in Bishopsgate Street. The hall lay at the back of a courtyard entered from the street; behind it lay gardens and further courts.

1 Hall
2 Parlour
3 Court
4 Garden
5 Back gate
6 Houses on street

retained one wing of the earlier house to form the southern range of a courtyard entered from the street via a passage under six tenements. The hall and parlour block were of ashlar-fronted brick on brick undercrofts. A semi-octagonal oriel window at the dais end of the hall incorporated Crosby's crest in its stone vault. The hall and upper parlour had richly gilded and ornamented timber ceilings, and behind the main house lay gardens and a private gate to St Helen's church, where Crosby and his wife lie in their own chapel. The hall may have been built, like that of Eltham Palace which it resembles, by the king's mason, Thomas Jurdan.

ELTHAM PALACE

Eltham Palace is a moated royal palace, originally in the countryside some miles from London or Westminster. The house was built by Bishop Bek of Durham in about 1300; parts of the wall on the inside of the moat probably date from his time. The palace passed to the crown in 1311 and several kings used it. Edward IV built the hall we see today in 1479, and Henry VII and Henry VIII added appartments and the chapel which figure in the exposed foundations. The splendid hammer-beam roof, by the King's Carpenter Edmund Gravely, sits stylistically half way between the roofs of Westminster Hall (1400) and Hampton Court (1515). A plan of the palace as it existed in 1616 shows the full extent of this royal country seat.

Plan of Eltham Palace, Eltham, Kent: rebuilt by Edward IV, and later by Henry VII and Henry VIII. In its final form it comprised a 15th-century bridge over a moat (1) leading to a large courtyard (2) with the Great Hall (3) dividing this space from the more private service rooms and kitchens (4) beyond. Henry VII added further royal apartments (5) and Henry VIII built the chapel (6). The roof of the hall is a fine example of the hammer-beam type (left); the hammer-beams are those which project horizontally out from the top of the wall.

1 Rafter
2 Collar
3 Brace
4 Hammer-beam

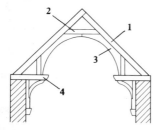

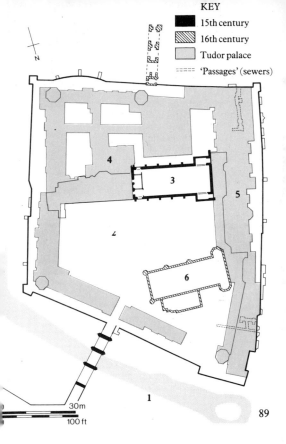

KEY

██ 15th century

▨ 16th century

▓ Tudor palace

‑ ‑ ‑ ‑ 'Passages' (sewers)

N

4

3

5

2

6

1

30m

100 ft

89

MEDIEVAL PARISH CHURCHES

Today only five medieval (pre-1540) churches remain in the City. Two of these (St Olave Hart Street and All Hallows Barking, Byward Street) were badly bombed in the War. Thus the remaining three – St Ethelburga, St Andrew Undershaft and St Helen Bishopsgate – must stand as representatives of the 107 churches which once thronged London's busy streets.

They each represent a different kind of church. St Ethelburga in Bishopsgate Street is a small medieval church dating from about 1400, with a nave and only a single aisle. Its squat tower once supported a small timber spire. In contrast, St Andrew Undershaft in Leadenhall Street (its name referring to the maypole or shaft which was erected nearby each year) is a church rebuilt through the generosity of one rich donor, merchant tailor Stephen Jennings, in 1520-32. The tower, its door and the lion's head knocker on it, are however from the 15th century.

But the best impression of a medieval London church is gained

Parish boundary marks, once a common sight on City buildings. These mark the boundaries of the parishes of St John the Baptist, St Mary-le-Bow, and St Mary-le-Strand.

The seal of the parish of St Mary-le-Bow, 1580, showing the pre-Fire church tower. The arched coronet on the tower (from the original Norman arches) was imitated by Wren in the present church.

inside St Helen Bishopsgate, which was both a nunnery and a parish church. This church has two naves, which were originally divided by a screen: the nuns worshipped in the northern part. Here can still be seen the stair to their dormitory, and a window or squint into the church from the sacristy or muniment

Interior of St Helen's church, Bishopsgate. In the medieval period this was a nunnery church with parishioners; the nuns worshipped in the north aisle (left) and were separated from the parishioners by screens which ran between these pillars. The church was rebuilt in 1475, partly with money from Sir John Crosby.

room. The nunnery buildings to the north of the church have now vanished. The south wall of the church is the oldest part, dating from the 12th century. From the outside, windows and a doorway can be discerned in the stonework. The church was rebuilt by Sir John Crosby (see pp. 86-7) in the late 15th century. He lies in a chapel at the east end. Smaller monuments, many brought from the nearby demolished church of St Martin Outwich, include stone and brass memorials. The larger tombs include those of Sir William Pickering, Ambassador to Spain under Elizabeth I (died 1574) and Sir Andrew Judd (died 1558), whose worldwide travels are recorded on his memorial. The brasses are particularly interesting, and include two 15th-century priests and Robert Rochester, Sergeant of the Pantry to Henry VIII. Fragments of medieval stained glass can be seen near Crosby's tomb; and a famous temporary resident in the parish in 1597, William Shakespeare, is commemorated in a window in the north wall presented to the church by an American in 1884.

WESTMINSTER ABBEY

Edward the Confessor, whose death in 1065 prompted the Norman invasion, built a royal palace alongside a monastery, the origins of which are wrapped in mystery, confused by a certain amount of monastic forgery of ancient charters. The Abbey may have been founded or refounded by king Offa in the 8th century, and by the 11th century, it was the seventh richest in the country. Fragments of the Saxon abbey, which Edward rebuilt, have been located in excavations and these, together with the representation on the Bayeux tapestry (see pp. 40-1) form a picture of a fine Romanesque church which was as modern as any in Normandy at the time. During the 12th century the abbey grew in prominence, partly because it established a cult of Edward the Confessor as a saint and attracted pilgrims to his tomb.

A tour of Westminster Abbey should begin in the church, then move to the cloister, the chapter house and the Dean's House, and end with more recent monuments such as Poets' Corner.

The west front of Westminster Abbey. Though the towers were skilfully added by Nicholas Hawksmoor in the 18th century, the lower parts are medieval; the work of Henry Yevele, the most famous medieval architect of England.

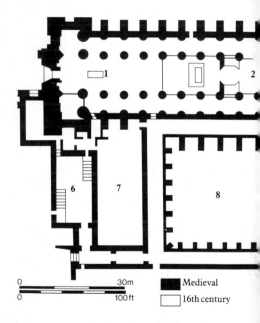

Plan of Westminster Abbey, illustrating the main parts. Monastic buildings such as the dormitory, frater (dining room), and hospital lay to the south and east. The Almoner's range later became the basis of Westminster School. The building history of the church itself divides into four main

N

1

2

6   7   8

0 _____ 30m
0 _____ 100ft

■ Medieval
□ 16th century

sections: the main part of the church in 1245-69; the western part of the nave, between 1375 and 1506; Henry VII's chapel, begun in 1503; and the western towers, added in 1734-40. The monastic buildings – the cloister, chapter house, infirmary and other parts – date largely from the Middle Ages.

1 Grave of the Unknown Warrior
2 Choir
3 Chapel of St Edward
4 Chapel of Henry VII
5 Poets' Corner
6 Dean's Court
7 Deanery
8 Cloisters
9 Chapter house
10 Chapel of the Pyx

Looking down the nave of Westminster Abbey towards the east end. In the 13th century architects and patrons (in this case the king) were much influenced by French models; hence the resemblance to a French cathedral. The plain stone surfaces would have been painted white with red lines to imitate stones, and red rosettes; the Purbeck pillars stayed their natural black. Medieval churches were always much more colourful than we think.

The structure of Westminster Abbey is best appreciated by standing near the crossing of the transepts and turning round slowly. Towards the east end, the vaulting directs its weight gracefully to the long marble shafts which are held to the walls and piers. Between the shafts are clearstorey or clerestory windows, each designed with two lancets and a circle. Below them lies the triforium, its tracery designed on the same principles. The 13th-century parts of the nave have a diaper pattern, whereas the 15th-century work has a plain surface.

In the south transept is a rose window, filling the gable end of the transept. This feature is more general in France than in England, but St Paul's cathedral had one in its east end, and for a time in the 14th century fashionable shoes had 'rose window' designs in leather on their uppers.

The burial place of monarchs

When Henry III erected a new shrine for the bones of the saintly king, Edward the Confessor, in 1269, he engaged artists from Rome who not only built and adorned the

The effigy in white marble of Queen Elizabeth I, who died in 1603.

tomb, but covered the floor of the saint's chapel with a mosaic in the style known as Cosmatesque from the Cosmati family of artists.

Succeeding monarchs followed Henry's example and turned the Abbey church into a royal mausoleum. Henry's own tomb (1272) and that of Queen Eleanor of Castile (1290) incorporate gilded effigies, the work of the London goldsmith William Torel. Other royal effigies include Edward III (died 1377),

Richard II (1399) and his queen, Anne of Bohemia (1394). On Edward III's tomb are small standing figures of 'weepers', representing his children.

Other tombs of note include those of William de Valence (1296), half-brother of Henry III, which has an effigy of oak covered with thin bronze plates enamelled probably at Limoges; and Aymer de Valence (1324), with its gabled canopy of stone with figures of earls on horseback. The grille over the Eleanor tomb, made in 1294, is a fine piece of medieval wrought ironwork.

Effigy of Henry III. The tomb-chest includes work in mosaic by the Italian Cosmati family.

The Chapter house

The chapter house must be approached from the cloister through a pillared passage, made low because the monks' dormitory or dorter lay overhead. The chapter house is a restoration of a building of about 1250. The vault of the roomy octagon is gathered in a central cluster of delicate marble shafts. All the wall space between the angle piers is filled with a large stained glass window; this grace is made possible by the formidable flying buttresses that support the building outside. Around the wall is a stone bench with arcading above it.

The floor of the chapter house is covered with decorated floor tiles bearing, among other things, the royal arms, legendary figures, fish, and the motto *Ut rosa flos florum sic est domus ista domorum* – 'as the rose is among flowers, so is this house among buildings'.

The chapter-house of Westminster Abbey, dating from the middle of the 13th century. The abbey and the nearby royal palace must have been a magnet for talented craftsmen. The glazed tile floor (below) is a unique example of its kind; its author unknown, but called The Westminster Tiler.

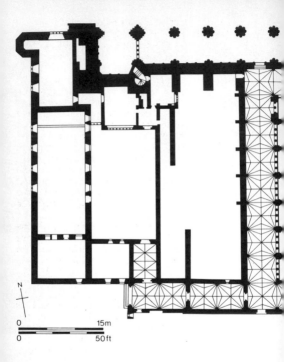

0
15m

0
50ft

104

Plan of the Dean's House, Westminster, showing its medieval origins; a hall entered by steps from a court-yard, a parlour and chamber at the 'high' end of the hall; the kitchen at the other end.

1 Nave of Abbey church
2 Hall
3 Courtyard
4 Kitchen
5 Jerusalem Chamber
6 Jericho Parlour
7 Cloisters

The Dean's House

Few visitors to Westminster Abbey realise, as they stand outside the west front, that next to them is a complete example of a 14th-century English house-complex. The Dean's House is found by going through the cloister. Like many medieval houses in London, it has a courtyard with the hall forming one side. It still keeps its open roof and 14th-century windows. At the south end of the hall, three doorways lead to what would have been the kitchen, buttery and pantry. The Jerusalem Chamber and the Jericho Parlour were added in the 16th century.

Before the Reformation, Westminster was a Benedictine abbey and the Dean's House was the Abbot's house. Although closely connected with the monarchy, the abbey was still a living and working monastery. Monks worked in the cloister (which had glazed windows on the inner sides), or in the subsidiary buildings such as the bakehouse, brewhouse, school and stables which are now beneath surrounding streets. The abbey garden, to the west of the cloister, is

105

one of the oldest in England.

A medieval Westminster monk's day started at midnight with the Night Office, divided into Matins and Lauds: between one and two and a half hours of half-standing, half-sitting and singing psalms. Hence the value of the misericords, the tip-up wooden choir stall seats which could be leant against. Prime, a short service of half an hour, followed at about 6 a.m. Then almost immediately came the Morrow Mass and the Chapter, held in the Chapter House. This could involve announcements for the day, a reading, an address by the abbot, and sessions of self-criticism. Work followed until the Sung Mass, and then dinner at about midday. Work then lasted until Vespers, a reading of a spiritual book, followed by supper (at about 5 p.m.), Compline and bed between 7 and 8 p.m. Like all medieval time-arranging, the timetable fitted the natural day and expanded or contracted in length with the season.

Poets' Corner

Before leaving Westminster Abbey one should sample the wide variety of other monuments which crowd into the church. Near the tomb of Elizabeth I in Henry VII's chapel is Innocents' Corner, so called because it contains a monument to the murdered Princes Edward V and Richard of York, his brother; and the tombs of two daughters of James I – Sophia, who died when only three days old in 1606, and Mary, who died aged two in 1607.

The east aisle of the south transept is known as Poets' Corner. Since a monument to Chaucer was erected here in 1556, monuments have been erected to great men of literature – Shakespeare, Milton, Wordsworth, Keats and Shelley among them. The inscription on Ben Jonson's monument reads *Orare Ben Jonson* – 'pray for Ben Jonson' – or, since there is a gap between the first two letters, it could simply be the English 'O rare Ben Jonson'. Elsewhere are monuments to eminent politicians, including Pitt, Gladstone and Churchill.

In Innocents' Corner in the abbey, Princess Mary, who died in 1607 aged two, looks over to Princess Sophia, her sister, who died in 1606 aged only three days. Both were daughters of James I. Child mortality, even among royalty, was high.

WESTMINSTER PALACE

The historical development of Westminster Palace is shown on the following pages. In 1100, when Rufus built the first Westminster Hall, the site was surrounded by marsh. In later centuries, especially in the major rebuilding under Richard II (in 1394-1402), the Palace expanded over land reclaimed from the marshes and the Thames. Thus, by the end of the middle ages, the Palace comprised a rambling complex of buildings of many different periods.

The conspirators in the Gunpowder Plot. Guy Fawkes is the third from the right.

Robert Winter Christopher Wright John Wright Thomas Percy Guido Fawkes Robert Catesby Thomas Winter

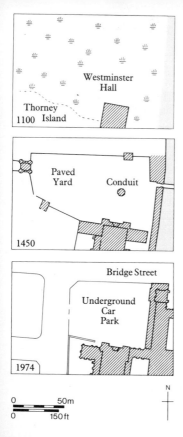

Left, *the main stages in the growth of Westminster Palace. In 1100 (top) William Rufus's hall must have jutted into the marsh surrounding Thorney Island. By 1450 (middle), the marsh had become a yard for the crowds thronging around the workshops and offices of the palace. In 1974 (bottom), excavation of an underground car park destroyed this vital area, mostly without record.*
Right: *plan of the Palace:*

1 Jewel Tower
2 Queen's Chapel and Chamber
3 Site of the Privy Palace
4 Painted Chamber
5 Lesser or White Hall
6 St Stephen's Chapel
7 Chapter House
8 St Stephen's Cloister
9 Vicars' houses
10 The Great Hall
11 Receipt of Exchequer
12 Inner Gateway
13 Exchequer
14 Site of kitchen

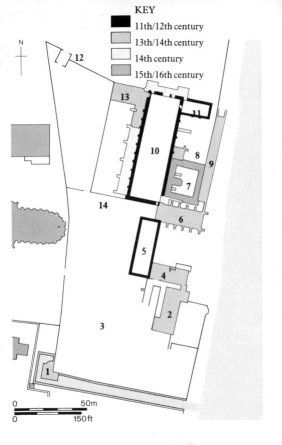

KEY

■ 11th/12th century

▨ 13th/14th century

□ 14th century

▧ 15th/16th century

N

12

13

11

10

8

9

14

7

6

5

4

2

3

1

0   50m

0   150ft

TUDOR, STUART AND RENAISSANCE LONDON (1500-1666)

The century and a half from 1500 is one of the periods of greatest change in the architecture of London. First, the monarchs Henry VII and (especially) Henry VIII built fine palaces such as Hampton Court. Then Henry VIII dissolved the monasteries and released much land in and around the capital for house-hungry immigrants from the rest of the country and abroad. In the later 16th and 17th centuries, many fine houses were built by the nobility and rising gentry. And from the opening of the 17th century classical influences began to make an appearance, particularly in the work of Inigo Jones.

We start at the final major addition to Westminster Abbey (apart from the west towers added by Hawksmoor in the 18th century). Henry VII's chapel (1509, built by

Panels in bronze from the gates to Henry VII's chapel, Westminster Abbey. They are vigorous designs in pierced bronze, representing the rival roses of York and Lancaster under a crown, the initials of the king, and royal symbols such as the falcon.

Henry VIII, originally as a mausoleum for his parents) is a treasure house of Tudor craftsmanship. The woodcarver's skill is shown in the canopies of the stalls, and the bronzework is some of the most skilful ever produced in this country. The tomb is the work of Pietro Torregiano, an Italian who reputedly once broke Michaelangelo's nose in a fight. The tomb is a mixture of English and Italian elements. As in previous centuries, the king and his queen lie in effigy, but the details are Italian: the medallions, wreaths of fruit and flowers, and the child angels or amorini on the corners. The screen which encloses the tomb has windows and tracery in bronze, with finely cast figures of saints in niches. The gates of oak are covered in bronze panels secured with bolts, the heads of which are in the form of a Tudor rose. Above is the lace-like fan vault, a structural masterpiece.

Here also are many *misericords*, beneath which are carvings of monsters, monkeys, David and Goliath, a Wife beating her Husband, the Judgment of Solomon and a Mermaid and Merman.

TUDOR PALACES

In a comparatively unified kingdom there was now no need for a fortified castle, though it was still the fashion to have large gateway towers. Henry VIII built several palaces in the London area, including two that can be seen today: St James's (still a royal residence) and Hampton Court. St James's, built on the site of a hospital in 1536,

View of St James's Palace in the time of Queen Anne, from an old engraving. Henry VIII rebuilt the dissolved hospital of St James for leper maidens into a palace in the 1530s.

The Great Gatehouse of Hampton Court, c 1536, built first by Cardinal Wolsey and augmented by Henry VIII. The fashionable brick facade has stone 'dressings' - corner stones (quoins), windows and doorways.

has been much altered, but the gatehouse and the Chapel Royal, with a ceiling painted by Holbein in 1540, remain.

A much better idea of a Tudor royal palace can be obtained by visiting Hampton Court in Middlesex, which Henry and his courtiers would have reached by river.

The buildings around the Base Court are those of the household and servants, low and simply treated.

Ahead lie buildings of more important character; the Great Hall, within the Clock Court, and other state rooms. The terracotta medallions are the work of Italian craftsmen, and the roof of the hall resembles those of contemporary French churches. But most of the palace is in English style, of brick with stone dressings. Above the roofs rise chimneys in groups, joined by their capitals and bases. Much of the brick was made in temporary kilns on or near the site.

Hampton Court includes Cardinal Wolsey's Closet, a rare survival of a Tudor interior. The walls are lined with linenfold panelling – the panels are carved with a treatment suggesting the folds of linen. The closet also has a curious and rich ceiling, of panels filled with Italian decoration in papier-mâché work.

THE INNS OF COURT

Other traces of Tudor and Elizabethan London survive in some of the buildings of the Inns of Court, where lawyers were (and still are) trained. The gatehouse of Lincoln's

Moulded bricks used to good effect in the chimneys of Hampton Court in the 1530s.

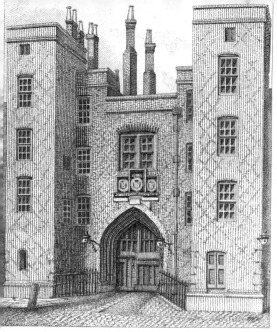

Gatehouse in Chancery Lane of Lincoln's Inn, built in 1518.

Inn (1518) resembles those of the royal palaces. Behind the gatehouse are courtyards with staircases in octagonal brick turrets in the corners, and a hall, built originally in

117

1493. The atmosphere is very like that of an Oxford or Cambridge college. At Middle Temple, the Hall was rebuilt in 1566-73. Here another architectural style can be seen making its first marks in the capital. The first wave of Renaissance decoration had embellished the houses and tombs of Henry's courtiers but had otherwise made little impact. In the 1560s, many Netherlandish refugees fled from their war-torn homeland to England, and brought a new style of continental decoration with them. This is shown in the screen at Middle Temple Hall (1566), carved with classical figures, lions' heads and designs called strapwork.

Coats of arms of donors to the rebuilding of Middle Temple Hall in the 16th century, set into the windows of the Hall. Private donations for the construction of important secular buildings were a civic and social duty.

SHAKESPEARE'S LONDON

The grasshopper symbol of Thomas Gresham, one of the greatest Elizabethan businessmen. It is still to be seen in Lombard Street, near the site of the Exchange he founded in 1570. Bronze grasshoppers adorned the skyline of his new building.

Another indication of London's close connection with the Low Countries, and with Antwerp in particular, is the first Royal Exchange (1569), built by the international businessman Thomas Gresham. It was based on the Bourse (an open-air meeting place for merchants) in Antwerp. An earlier import of classical ideas in the grand house of Protector Somerset in the Strand (1549) had only caught on among a small coterie of courtiers. But now, stylistic features such as open colonnades, statues in niches and plain brick facades with windows and doorways in simulated stonework, were transplanted from the Continent and began to spread.

The predominant building materials were still however timber, lath and plaster. Although they are both heavily restored, the facades of Staple Inn in Holborn and Prince Henry's Room in Fleet Street give a good impression of Tudor buildings in London. The Staple Inn frontage was built in 1586. Its attic storey is raised on small side walls, to win more space in the overcrowded city.

119

The close-studding (where the vertical timbers or studs are set close together) may, however, be a modern feature. Old photographs show that the framing was simply arranged in rectangular panels. The windows are similarly nearly all modern copies of Tudor work.

Prince Henry's room in Fleet Street had to be moved back a few feet when the road was widened early in the 20th century. Its exterior shows strapwork panels and the balustrade in the attic storey is a feature once very common among the timber-framed houses of London. Inside, on the first floor, is a small museum in a room with a rich plaster ceiling of about 1610. And though the Prince of Wales' feathers feature in the ceiling, this is likely to

The City of London from the south: a woodcut panorama, dating from about 1560. St Paul's still has its spire, which was damaged by lightning in 1561 and taken down. The cosmopolitan city was still medieval in

appearance, cut off from the surrounding fields by the city walls. Note how larger ships are contained in The Pool below London Bridge; the draw-bridge in the bridge had stopped working around 1500.

be a reference to a street sign of that name rather than to the Prince at the time, Prince Henry (son of James I).

Once there were many galleried inns in London, especially on the approach roads to the city. The only survivor is the George Inn, a short way south of London Bridge. Even here only one wing remains; originally the Inn had a narrow yard surrounded by galleries. The surviving wing was built in 1677 after a serious fire in Southwark. As oak was becoming scarce, the frame is of softwood in a brick carcase. The original partitions dividing the attic into rooms for travellers still exist. In yards such as this, Shakespeare would have staged his plays, the audience looking down from these galleries.

The frontage to Holborn of Staple Inn, dating originally from 1586. Such facades of shops were common in London streets, screening large houses behind (in this case, an Inn of lawyers). The appearance owes much to restorations of 1894 and 1936; originally the houses were probably framed in panels, not the close-studding (close-set timbers) shown here.

INIGO JONES

Inigo Jones was born in 1573. As a young man, he travelled widely to study European architecture, particularly the classical constructions of Andreas Palladio, which were then the newest fashion in such places as Vicenza in northern Italy. Jones worked for the Court, first as a masque designer and then as Surveyor (or architect).

His first building as Surveyor was the Queen's House at Greenwich (1616-35), originally meant to be a small pleasure-house in two sections

South face of the Queen's House, Greenwich. The loggia on the first floor, the rusticated ground floor and the low roof fronted by a balustrade were all new elements, imported by Jones from Italy.

124

flanking a road marking the boundary between Greenwich Palace and Greenwich Park. The road passed under the house along the line now marked by colonnades on each side. The house, the first in England designed fully in the Italian manner, has a loggia facing south, instead of north as it would have done in Italy. Contemporaries called the house 'a curious devise'. Inside, the hall rises through both storeys, and the rooms open off one another.

In 1619 Jones began work on the Banqueting House in Whitehall, which was finished by 1622. Like

Plan of the Queen's House, originally spanning the Dover road. Webb filled in the bridging parts later.
1 Salon (upper part)
2 Courts
3 Loggia
4 Queen's chambers

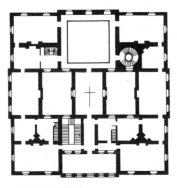

The Banqueting
House, Whitehall
(1619). Note the
alternating curved
and triangular pedi-
ments to the windows,
and the swags of
ornament beneath the
balustrade.

the Queen's House, its design is
based upon Jones's knowledge of
Palladian buildings in Italy. It is in
the form of a double cube, with a
hall rising through two storeys. The
ceiling, by Peter Paul Rubens, is
called The Apotheosis of James I
(1634). James, the father of Charles
I, the reigning monarch, is shown
among figures of Justice, Zeal,
Religion, Honour and Victory.
Ironically it was from a first-floor
window of this very building that
Charles I was to step out to his own
execution in 1649.

During the first half of the 17th
century' the open land between the
City and Westminster was also
changing character. The old bishops' palaces along the Strand had
fallen into the hands of courtiers
who rebuilt them in Elizabethan
style with classical trimmings. From
these urban palaces, they went back
and forth to court by river. The
watergate of the Duke of York
(1626), now marooned in gardens on
the Embankment, shows where the
river bank formerly lay.

In the 1630s Inigo Jones laid out
Covent Garden, a speculative development by the Duke of Bedford

whose house lay on the south side. The square or piazza was influenced both by Italian practice and by the Place de Royale (now Place des Vosges) in Paris. Terraces of brick houses with a ground-floor colonnade or loggia occupied two sides of the square, while the remaining side was taken up with a church for the new residents, St Paul Covent Garden (later damaged by fire and rebuilt, but substantially as Jones intended). Covent Garden was meant to be an aristocratic, or at

The Duke of York's watergate (1626), now in a garden on the Embankment; but originally on the bank of the Thames, where the Duke's personal barge would arrive at his London residence.

The front of Lindsey House, Lincoln's Inn Fields; an engraving which shows its original aspect, before the windows were increased in size and the single doorway made into two.

least high-quality, suburb. It became a vegetable market only later when fashion had moved even further westwards, and had to wait until the 20th century to regain its former appeal

A house of 1640, built by Jones or by some close colleague, can still be found in altered form at Lindsey House, 59-60 Lincoln's Inn Fields (another greenfield site, laid out in 1638-58). The double or giant order Corinthian pilasters were imitated on some of London's timber-framed houses of the same time, and the architraves above the windows give the first hint of the styles that were to be followed by Christopher Wren and his generation.

129

HOUSES AROUND LONDON

In the 1630s, and perhaps slightly before, a number of important brick houses were built in the countryside around London. The best example, and the earliest, is the Dutch House or Kew Palace of 1631, now within the Royal Botanic Gardens at Kew. This was built by Simon Fortrey, a London merchant of Dutch descent. The gables have double-curved profiles and the windows have pediments which are alternately triangular and segmental, as at the Banqueting House. Similar houses of certain prominent merchants and other wealthy individuals are found at Charlton in southeast London, in Highgate and in Middlesex.

Within the narrow street frontages of the City, there was very little of this new styling in brick, perhaps because much of the City property was held on lease from the ancient livery companies. And so the City remained obstinately timber-framed, congested and insanitary, a natural prey to the ever-present threat of pestilence and the accidental disaster of fire.

The garden front of Kew Palace (1631), originally the country houses of a London merchant. The terrace with a loggia in the centre is a feature of the most up-to-date houses of the time, including some in the City.

THE
GREAT FIRE AND
SIR CHRISTOPHER
WREN (1666-1710)

At about 3 a.m. on the morning of Sunday the 2nd of September 1666, a middle-aged civil servant called Samuel Pepys was called from his bed by a maid, who pointed out a fire somewhere to the west of his house near the Tower of London. He did not think much of it, and went back to sleep. In the morning, however, he found that much of the area around the bridge, centred on Pudding Lane, was laid waste and the fire was still spreading. He took a boat up under the bridge, and saw people flinging goods into boats, or into the river. As the fire spread, they clambered from one river stair to another, moving their possessions again and again, to avoid the advancing flames.

By the end of the day the fire appeared as an arch of flame a mile long. It raged for five days, until the wind finally changed and some houses were blown up to create firebreaks in Fleet Street and West Smithfield. The devastation stretched from the Tower to the Temple, and from the riverside to St Giles Cripplegate in the north.

The Great Fire is thought to have started in a baker's house in

Pudding Lane (at a commemoration ceremony in 1986, the Bakers' Company formally expressed 'regret'). The Monument to the fire stands near its source. It was built in 1671-7 to the design of Christopher Wren. Originally there were to be brass flames issuing from loopholes along its entire height and a phoenix at the top. The Latin inscription on the north side records the disaster: it consumed 89 churches, the City gates, St Paul's, Guildhall, many public structures, 13,200 houses, and left 436 acres of the City in ruins. The inscription on the south side records the rebuilding of London, aided by taxes on, of all things, coal. On the west front a relief by Caius Cibber shows both destruction and restoration in allegory. A female figure representing the City of London sits disconsolately on a pile of ruins. Time tries to raise her up; behind are goddesses of Plenty and Peace. A beehive at the City's feet symbolises hard work; below, the dragon from the City arms tries to hold up the ruins. King Charles II, attended by Architecture and Liberty, directs Science who holds Nature in her hand.

Above, *the Fat Boy at the corner of Giltspur Street marks the spot, originally known as Pie Corner (from the shop sign of a Magpie), where the Great Fire was halted in 1666.*
Right, *the base of the Monument at the turn of this century.*

134

THE MONUMENT is OPEN to the PUBLIC
from 9 a.m. to 6 p.m. from March 10 to Sept. 30
and from Sept. 30 to the 10 of March 9 to 5
ADMISSION 3d EACH PERSON

·135

The west facade of St Paul's Cathedral. The Cathedral is 555 ft long and the top of the dome 366 ft high. The west facade and its towers show Wren's sympathy with Continental Baroque churches. The dome is a descendant of that designed by Bramante for St Peter's Rome.

Christopher Wren (1632-1723) was a scientific genius for whom architecture was only one branch of learning. Although he continued the classical trends of Inigo Jones, he also borrowed freely from French and Dutch models in his churches and public buildings. He and his masons transformed the appearance of the city with widespread use of brick and Portland stone. Wren's work includes a Renaissance cathedral, 52 parish churches (of which 24 survive, many restored after World War II, along with the towers of six others), two important hospitals at Chelsea and Greenwich, extensive building at Hampton Court, and many other buildings.

St Paul's cathedral took 35 years to build, from 1675 to 1710. In plan it is a Latin cross, with a dome raised upon a drum over the central crossing where a tower would be in a medieval cathedral. We are so used to its appearance today that it requires an effort to appreciate how novel it was in its mixture of styles. The exterior wall facades recall Inigo Jones' work (compare the

137

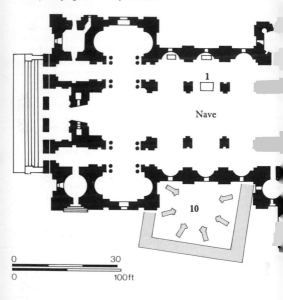

Plan of St Paul's Cathedral, finished in 1710. Christopher Wren was buried in the crypt beneath in 1723; also lying there are the Duke of Wellington and Lord Nelson. The famous Whispering Gallery runs round the inside of the dome.

Nave

1

10

0 — 30
0 — 100 ft

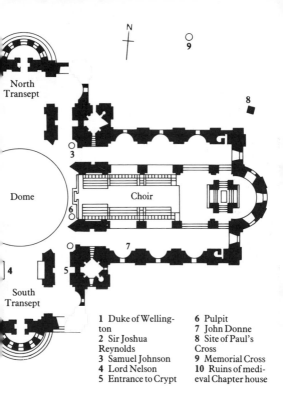

N

North
Transept

Dome

Choir

South
Transept

1 Duke of Welling-
ton
2 Sir Joshua
Reynolds
3 Samuel Johnson
4 Lord Nelson
5 Entrance to Crypt

6 Pulpit
7 John Donne
8 Site of Paul's
Cross
9 Memorial Cross
10 Ruins of medi-
eval Chapter house

Banqueting House) and Italian palaces. The transepts to north and south have ornate porches borrowed from contemporary churches in Rome. The west end comprises a two-storeyed portico with a sculptured pediment showing the Conversion of St Paul (in Continental baroque style), and two many-columned towers which were repeated, with variations, in Wren's parish-church towers throughout the city. Like the lantern above the dome, they are modelled on little classical temples, though they are Christian church towers.

Inside the cathedral, look out for the monuments of benefactors of the English nation, which began to appear in the cathedral after 1794. In side chapels and on walls may be found monuments to great military leaders such as Lord Kitchener and the Duke of Wellington; Nelson's urn (which reuses the urn originally made for Cardinal Wolsey) now lies in the crypt. Samuel Johnson stands in Roman costume, with bare chest and legs; diagonally opposite him is Sir Joshua Reynolds.

In the crypt, among many other monuments, is one of black marble

The church of St Magnus the Martyr, Thames Street; Wren borrowed the design of the tower from the Low Countries.

to Wren himself, with the inscription *Si monumentum requiris, circumspice* – 'If you seek a monument, look around you.'

The Cathedral's outer dome, made of timber and lead, is carried on a brick cone. The interior dome is built within this cone, its lower part forming the drum that lights the crossing by means of a series of windows screened on the outside by a colonnade. The internal dome is actually much lower than the exterior dome. In similar fashion, the side walls of the church rise much higher than the roof so that they mask it; they are blank facades. The result is an illusion of height, enhancing the monumental aspect of the building from all viewpoints.

WREN'S PARISH CHURCHES

The parish churches rebuilt by Wren and his craftsmen are large, clean rooms for preaching and listening, lit by big windows and decorated originally in simple manner with white plasterwork and gold leaf. Wren would not have approved of the stained glass which now

141

adorns many of his churches.

Two examples show the variety of Wren's sources. At St Mary-le-Bow, the design of the steeple recalls the pre-Fire church. The body of the church may derive from the Basilica of Maxentius in the Roman Forum, and the elaborate exterior doorway of the tower is based on that of a Parisian house built in 1611, the Hotel de Conti. The tower of St Magnus the Martyr in Thames Street shows different influences: it is based on the baroque tower and steeple of St Charles Borromee in Antwerp, though the elaborate decoration has been simplified.

Besides walking the streets of the City to visit the remaining Wren churches, the visitor can try to identify them from some high vantage point such as the top of the Monument or one of the modern office blocks. Look out for the vanes and finials which crown the steeples. St Lawrence Jewry has a gridiron, the emblem of St Lawrence; St Peter Cornhill has the key of its saint. St Mary-le-Bow has a dragon from the City Arms. Several of the other churches merely have a simple ball and vane.

Plan of the Royal Hospital, Greenwich; one of the few building complexes to be laid out in the late 17th-century French (Parisian) fashion in London. It is a fine example of what can be called an English Renaissance design.
1 King Charles's Block
2 Queen Anne's Block
3 King William's Block
4 Queen Mary's Block
5 The Queen's House
6 National Maritime Museum

KEY

early 17th century

early 18th

mid-late 18th

19th century

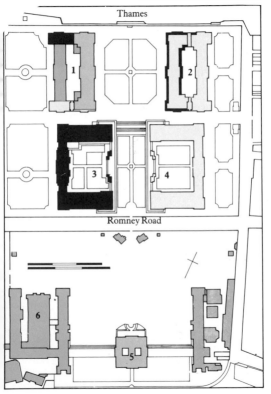

GREENWICH HOSPITAL

Thames

Romney Road

1

2

3

4

6

5

GREENWICH HOSPITAL AND OTHER BUILDINGS

Wren's Naval Hospital at Green-wich, rebuilt from a royal palace, presents one of London's most memorable views when approached from the river. It has two domes: the western was built by Wren, and the

The waterfront view of the Royal Naval Hospital, Greenwich. Originally intended to be a royal palace, it became a Naval Hospital in the spirit of the Invalides,

eastern by his pupil Hawksmoor. Wren intended to complete the colonnades as far as the Queen's House, which was to be demolished in favour of a chapel with a third dome of loftier proportions. Fortunately for subsequent generations, the plan was not carried out, but we must admit that there does

seem to be a hole in the middle of the view. Greenwich, like Wren's other hospital at Chelsea, shows a new concern with magnificent and orderly planning of the site and setting.

Wren built much more in and around London during his long life. He added south and east wings to the royal palace at Hampton Court for William and Mary in 1689-94, in the style of a Baroque schloss or palace such as the Louvre. The original intention was to rebuild all of Henry VIII's palace. The east and

The east front of Hampton Court by Christopher Wren; it resembles many country houses of the late 17th century, but critics say it is not quite as good as the French royal palace at Versailles.

Temple Bar, built by Wren, in its original site dividing Fleet Street from the Strand; from an old engraving. There are plans to bring Temple Bar back to a site near St Paul's.

south fronts are a noble attempt at palace architecture, but experts say they do not compare well with the Louvre or Versailles. One problem is that the central projection of pillars provides a good centre point to the facade in a horizontal direction, but the pediment should be at the very top of the design, not masked by the attic storey.

The Royal Military Hospital at Chelsea is laid out, like the naval hospital at Greenwich, with its principal front and noble portico towards the river. It is however less

147

ambitious in scale, and the materials and proportions give a more homely setting for its ex-servicemen inmates, the Chelsea Pensioners.

ORDINARY HOUSES

Many new streets and squares were laid out between the old City and Westminster as the increasing population of London demanded homes. Despite the rebuilding of large parts of the City, the emphasis of fashion moved inexorably westwards towards the court of Charles II, around Pall Mall and St James's. houses of this period have almost all been destroyed, but an impression of one can be gained from Dr Johnson's 18th-century house in Gough Square, off Fleet Street. The simple facade in a court, two or three storeys high, with sash windows, is in a style that traces its origins directly to the houses built in the 1670s, after the Great Fire.

The Great Fire, in effect, sanitised a large area of London, in that houses built afterwards were obliged to conform to strict building regulations.

Dr Johnson's House in Gough Square, north of Fleet Street. Built about 1700, it now holds a small museum of the great man's memorabilia; while living here between 1749 and 1755, Johnson compiled his Dictionary. In the 17th century many hundreds of courts would contain one large house like this and other smaller brick tenements.

The sign of the Boar's
Head, from East-
cheap, dated 1668.
After the Fire, inn
signs had to be flush
with the front of the
building.

149

GEORGIAN (1714-1830) LONDON

The Georgian period spans the reigns of all the four Georges. Throughout the period, Britain adopted a classical style in religious, public and domestic architecture which rapidly became standard. The style transformed London and many other towns.

HAWKSMOOR AND GIBBS

The period begins in London with two architects who were far from staid and decorous. The first was Nicholas Hawksmoor (1661-1736), the pupil and associate of Wren. In London he built the western towers of Westminster Abbey (1734) and six remarkable churches, of which the best surviving examples are St Mary Woolnoth (1716-26) and Christ Church, Spitalfields (1714-28).

The other architect was James Gibbs (1682-1754). As a Scot and

Christ Church, Spitalfields (1714-28), by Nicholas Hawksmoor.

St Mary Woolnoth (1716-26), King William Street, also by Hawksmoor. This has been called 'the most original church exterior in the City of London'; the interior, largely as left by Hawksmoor, is important because it is all of one piece — well worth a visit.

probably a Jacobite, he fell out of favour after the defeat of the Scottish rebellion in 1715, but his two best London works date from about this time: St Mary-le-Strand (1714-17) and St Martin-in-the-Fields (1720-6). St Mary-le-Strand carries on the Wren tradition with fresh innovation: it is the nearest thing in London to the baroque churches of Rome. St Martin-in-the-Fields is now very familiar, not

151

only because of its situation in Trafalgar Square but because it was widely imitated, especially in America and the West Indies. However, it is important to realise how revolutionary it was at the time, with its classical temple portico at the west end supporting a church spire in the gothic manner.

Gibbs was one of the defeated contestants in the competition to design a house for the Lord Mayor of London, the Mansion House, in

Above left: *St Martin-in-the-Fields (1722-6), by James Gibbs. The magnificent west front is reminiscent of a temple, with six Corinthian columns and a pediment.*
Above right: *St Mary-le-Strand (1714-17) by Gibbs, now on a fine site in the Strand.*

Mansion House (1739-53) in the City of London, from an old engraving. This shows the original extra storeys, known as the Mayor's Nest and Noah's Ark, which have fortunately been removed. Mansion House is the official residence of the Lord Mayor.

1739. The winner was George Dance the elder. The building is fronted with a portico of six Corinthian columns, supporting a pediment with a relief showing London trampling on Envy and leading in the spirit of Plenty. Originally, two attics rose above the roofline: they were popularly known as the Mayor's Nest and Noah's Ark. Inside is an Egyptian Hall, based on a description by the Roman architect Vitruvius.

BURLINGTON, CAMPBELL AND KENT

Lord Burlington (1694-1753) and his friend, Colin Campbell (d. 1729) were largely responsible for the Palladian revival in George I's reign (1714-27) which reasserted the classicism of Inigo Jones over the exuberance of Wren. Burlington used Campbell to help him design his house in Piccadilly, Burlington House, but only part of that survives, in altered form, as the Royal Academy. He also built his own villa at Chiswick (Chiswick House) basing it on several different Palladian designs.

Burlington's protégé, William

Chiswick House (1725-9), designed by Lord Burlington. This country villa was to be used for entertaining, as a library and art gallery. It is based largely on Palladio's Villa Capra near Vicenza in North Italy. Today it is managed by the Victoria & Albert Museum.

Below: *the main orders (types of column) of classical architecture, which were widely used in large Georgian buildings.*

A Greek Doric
B Roman Doric
C Tuscan Doric
D Ionic
E Corinthian
1 Cornice
2 Frieze
3 Architrave
4 Capital

Kent (c.1685-1748), emerged as an important figure in the revival in the 1730s. His Horse Guards' Parade (designed c.1745-8, built 1750-60), now facing the Banqueting House in Whitehall, demonstrates the new fashion. There are many projections, wings and arched passages, while the principal windows are in the shape called Venetian. But the imposing facade was hardly practical; of five Venetian windows facing the park, only one is in a principal room, the others being squeezed into the corners of small offices. The central driveway has an arch so low that Hogarth gleefully painted a coach emerging from it with a headless driver.

CHAMBERS AND ADAM

Below: the river front of Somerset House, dating from 1776–86. Right: the Pagoda in Kew Gardens, by Sir William Chambers (1761), a result of Chambers' travels in the Far East.

In the middle of the 18th century, two further architects who were destined to be influential returned from prolonged European study-tours. Sir William Chambers (1723-96) rebuilt Somerset House, formerly a royal palace, into a complex of buildings designed to hold the Royal Academy and various other learned bodies. Before the laying of the Embankment between it and the river, it was an even more imposing pile with massive water gates. Chambers was generally a staid classicist, but his pagoda at Kew (1761) is a fine example of the contemporary craze for *Chinoiserie* (the European version of Chinese style).

The other returning architect was Robert Adam (1728-92). Adam designed the Admiralty Screen in Whitehall in 1759-61, with Tuscan columns and two sea-horses rising above it. He is mainly known today, however, for his meticulous, cheerful interiors (such a welcome contrast, in the 1760s, to the Palladian dryness of the previous 30 years). He built several houses for clients in London, but they have largely been destroyed or altered.

THE GEORGIAN HOUSE

From the outside, Georgian
houses are simple, regular and
almost without decoration; within,
they strained for grace and elegance.
They were often built in blocks or
'rows' (such as Bedford Row,
Holborn or Cheyne Row, Chelsea).
Urban life encouraged the use of a
basement storey for servants, which
elevated the ground floor, and
therefore the front door, by several
feet above the pavement; a short
stair was therefore often necessary.
The door was often the only decorated element in the facade, except
perhaps for the graceful iron balustrade of a balcony. The effects of the
Great Fire were still being debated.
In 1707 cornices along the eaves,
made of wood, were banned; from
1709, the broad window frames that
used to be fixed flush with the
outside face of the wall had to be
recessed and, from 1774, the frames
were further hidden by being fitted
into recesses or reveals in the
window openings. The effect of a
Georgian house resides in the
balance of the windows and the
entrance, which is in the centre for

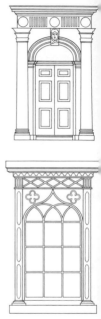

larger houses, but to one side in the smaller facades. Examples of fashionable houses, which did not disdain being part of a terrace, can be seen at 44 Berkeley Square (by William Kent, 1742-4), and 20 Portman Square (by Robert Adam, built in 1775-89).

Left *and* above: *window and door shapes from 18th-century houses in London.*
Right, *20 St James's Square, by Robert Adam (1775-89). The ground floor is rusticated (the courses emphasised by leaving out mortar pointing), and above rise two-storey pilasters (decorative 'columns'). Behind are handsome stables.*

HYDE PARK

Hyde Park, the largest park in London, was originally the property of Westminster Abbey. It became crown property at the Dissolution of

Constitution Arch, built in 1846, is now surmounted by an effigy of Victory in a chariot, dating from 1912.

the Monasteries. Henry VIII hunted deer here. It was first opened to the public in 1637. In 1730, the Serpentine was created by damming the Westbourne, a stream which flowed through it. Rotten Row derives its name from *route du roi*, the king's road through the park. During the 18th and 19th centuries, the park became the favourite site for duels; today duels of a verbal kind take place at Speakers's Corner, especially on Sundays.

Hyde Park Corner, though shaped awkwardly, was regarded as one of the main entrances to London from the 18th century, and several monuments are now to be found there. In 1825, Decimus Burton designed the Hyde Park Corner Screen and Constitution Arch, meant to be the grand exit from the park to Buckingham Palace. Originally, the arch was in line with the Screen, but it was moved to Constitution Hill in 1883, and given a bronze statue of Victory in a chariot in 1912. Nearby are monuments to the Duke of Wellington (close to his London residence, Apsley House) and the Royal Artillery Corps.

Speaker's Corner, at Marble Arch, a reminder of a tradition of relaxed tolerance in Hyde Park which dates back to Henry VIII.

JOHN NASH; REGENT STREET AND REGENT'S PARK

John Nash (1752-1835) designed many picturesque houses in gothic, Italianate and classical styles. Under the patronage of the Prince Regent, he showed himself to be a brilliant town-planner, conceiving the great sweep of Regent Street (1818) from the Prince's Carlton House in Pall

Cumberland Terrace (1826-7) by John Nash borders Regent's Park. It is based on palace architecture, but is meant to be contrasted with the natural landscape around it.

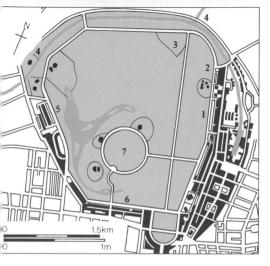

Map of Regent's Park showing the buildings associated with Nash:
1 Cumberland Terrace
2 Gloucester Gate
3 Zoo
4 Regent's Canal
5 Hanover Terrace
6 York Terrace
7 Botanic Gardens

Mall (now demolished) to Regent's Park (planned 1811-13, laid out in the 1820s). Regent Street has been largely rebuilt, but the monumental terraces around the Park, such as Cumberland Terrace, were among the most splendid of their time in Europe. Scattered throughout the Park are eight villas, only a small portion of the number that Nash had originally envisaged.

VICTORIAN LONDON:

THE EMPIRE (1820-1914)

The changes in London during the long reign of Victoria (1837-1901) were great and far-reaching. It became the biggest city in the world, at the hub of the greatest empire the world had seen. Victorian buildings reflected the wealth and confidence of an imperial power, as well as the exotic influences of its far-flung domains. There were appalling slums as well as great engineering achievements and modest housing for the growing middle classes as well as grandiose mansions and offices for the rich and powerful. Victorian London was diverse.

TRAFALGAR SQUARE

An open space in the area of Trafalgar Square was suggested by John Nash in 1812, and his proposal carried out in the 1820s. The square lies on a slope with the National

The statue of Nelson looks out towards the sea, embellished with a capstan and a coiled rope; the first plan was for it to be 200 ft high, not the eventual 124 ft. Around it Trafalgar Square was laid out, becoming one of the focal points of modern London.

Gallery (1832-8) on the north side. Apart from St Martin-in-the-Fields, nothing survives of the buildings which originally surrounded the square; Admiralty Arch to the west is of the Edwardian period (see p. 208). The open space is dominated by the 170-foot Nelson's Column (1839-42), with a 17-foot statue of England's naval hero on the top. The lions at the base, each 20 feet long, were added in 1858-67. By the north terrace is an equestrian statue of George IV, originally intended for Marble Arch. The pools were added only in 1939, and were the last work in London of the distinguished Edwin Lutyens.

BUCKINGHAM PALACE

The Duke of Buckingham built a country house near the fashionable part of London, around the court, in 1705. The Prince Regent asked John Nash to make it into a palace, which he began in 1826, but he was later disgraced and the palace was eventually finished to another design in 1837. Nash contrived to keep the rural atmosphere by retaining the private park and gardens at the rear. To the east, the side seen today by the public from the Mall, was a

The east facade of Buckingham Palace, looking down the Mall. It is a very English and rather stiff country house in the middle of the City. Behind are large private gardens where the Royal Garden Parties are held.

large courtyard eventually crossed by the wing of 1847 added by Queen Victoria. When it was built the original Marble Arch had to be moved to its present site. The facade facing the Mall was rebuilt in French style in 1913. The balcony was added in the space of four months at the request of George V. Though by no means brilliant as architecture, Buckingham Palace is notable for being the last example of large scale royal building work in London, closing (or perhaps just temporarily halting?) a tradition begun with the White Tower by William the Conqueror.

It is worth taking a look into the Royal Mews in Buckingham Palace Road, to the left of the main facade. Then retrace your steps to the Victoria Memorial (1911) in front of the palace, looking down the Mall. The memorial expresses much about Victoria and the society she governed. The Queen, carved from a single block of marble, is accompanied by Charity on the west side of the monument, Truth to the north and Justice to the south. Between them are ships' prows. Below, forming the outer balustrade, are mermaids and Progress and Peace, Manufacture and Agriculture, Painting and Architecture, Shipbuilding and Mining. On the top, 82 feet above the ground, is a gilt Victory.

On the second Saturday in June the Mall and the adjacent Horseguards' Parade, off Whitehall, are used for the 200-year old ceremony of the Trooping of the Colour. The

The Changing of the Guard at Buckingham Palace is one of London's traditional ceremonies that few visitors miss. It takes place most mornings in front of the Palace buildings.

Queen rides out from Buckingham Palace to inspect the Colours of a selected regiment. Originally this trooping took place so that the soldiers could recognise their own colours, a vital necessity in the smoke of battle.

The more common ceremony of Changing the Guard takes place in the forecourt of the Palace at 11.30 a.m. every day in summer, and on alternate days in winter.

MARBLE ARCH

Marble Arch was part of John Nash's design for Buckingham Palace, where it stood from 1828 to 1847. It was then ousted for the new

Marble Arch now sits in a traffic island, far from its original site in front of Buckingham Palace. Its marble faces have not weathered well and it looks out of place; but it goes well with the adjacent Speaker's Corner of Hyde Park.

east range of the palace and moved to its present site at Speaker's Corner, where Oxford Street meets Park Lane. The marble comes from Seravezza in Italy, and its three archways are reminiscent of the Arch of Constantine in the Roman forum. The theme of Victory is pursued in the sculptured reliefs around it, and a statue of Victory was originally intended to stand on the top. The position was actually taken by the equestrian statue of George IV which now stands in Trafalgar Square.

THE ALBERT MEMORIAL AND ALBERT HALL

A fine example of Victorian architecture is the group of buildings in South Kensington which are associated with Prince Albert, whose death in 1861 was to make Victoria a grieving widow for the rest of her long reign. The Albert Memorial was built in 1863-72 by Sir Gilbert Scott as a 'memorial of our blameless Prince'. The Queen herself selected Scott's design after a limited competition. The memorial cost as much as ten parish churches to build. The intention was to erect a ciborium, a shrine vaguely on medieval lines, to shelter a statue of Prince Albert, and embellish the shrine with sculptures, mosaics and bronze. It is imbued with the sprit of the Great Exhibition which was, dear to the Prince's heart (he is shown reading the Exhibition Catalogue). Similarly, the main decorative features were meant to be heavily allegorical. Around the base is a frieze depicting painters, poets composers, sculptors and architects (including Vanburgh, Palladio, and Pugin – with his back to the others). At the corners are marble groups representing Engineering, Agriculture, Manufacture and Commerce. Since the memorial is at the centre of the British Empire which covered the world, Europe, Africa, America and Asia are shown at the outer corners. On the east side was the original site of the Crystal Palace, erected for the Great Exhibition in 1851.

Nearby, the Royal Albert Hall (1867-71) is refreshingly plain by contrast. It is a domed brick cylinder 735 feet across with re-

Left: *Prince Albert, consort of Queen Victoria, is commemorated by a monument resembling a medieval shrine, normally built for the bones of saints.* Above: *the Albert Hall holds 8000 people – though its fame rest equally on the standing concert-goers who form the audience for the annual Promenade concerts.*

strained decoration in terra cotta and mosaic featuring the Triumph of Art and Letters. The designs for this frieze were enlarged by photography and then turned into ceramic mosaics.

A complex of cultural institutions lies south of the Albert Memorial. It includes the Royal School of Music, the Science Museum, the Natural History Museum and the Victoria and Albert Museum. Although some are of later dates, they occupy a site intended for educational uses after the Great Exhibition.

THE BRITISH MUSEUM

The largest museum building in London, however, lies across central London in Bloomsbury. The original British Museum was a 17th-century mansion, Montagu House. By 1800, this housed several notable collections of manuscripts, antiquities and paintings, which had been left to the nation. In 1816 the Elgin marbles, from the ancient Greek Parthenon temple in Athens, were added. Space rapidly became inadequate. Public museums and

The facade of the British Museum in Great Russell Street. The Museum now occupies an area of 11.3 acres. Like all great museums, it should be explored in several short visits.

In addition to its collections of arte-facts, drawings and paintings, the Museum houses the main collection of the British Library, in miles of underground corridors.

libraries were being built all over Europe at the time, and London was to be no exception. The architect, Robert Smirke, followed several contemporary European models (such as the Altes Museum in Berlin or the Parliament House in Dublin) in his design (1823-47), as well as paying homage to the world of classical learning.

The east wing was built first to house the King's library and is an early example of the use of spans of iron beams clad in concrete. The other wings followed, and the well

175

known front facade was erected in 1842-7. The original museum was a quadrangle around a courtyard, but the courtyard was filled in to form what is now the British Library in 1852-7 (designed by Smirke's younger brother Sydney). The famous dome of the Reading Room is larger than those of St Peter's in Rome or St Paul's in London and was clearly inspired by the slightly larger Pantheon in Rome.

There have been suggestions that the great colonnaded facade can only really be appreciated by clearing the smaller buildings away from in front of it, as far as the church of St George, by Hawksmoor, in Bloomsbury Way. But this would be a tragedy for the small-scale pubs, shops and dwellings which skirt the great institution of learning and treasure-house of the past.

Statue of King Richard I in front of the Houses of Parliament. The late 14th-century Westminster Hall, the historic centre of the complex, is on the left.

THE HOUSES OF PARLIAMENT

The British Museum is almost the last expression of the monumental classical style, which was fashionable in the opening decades of the 19th century. While the Museum

was being built, however, very different buildings were appearing to house the British Parliament at Westminster.

In October 1834 the old Palace of Westminster was largely destroyed by fire. Within a year, a competition to design a new Houses of Parliament had been announced; it was to be in a Gothic or Elizabethan style. The winning architect was Charles Barry, who was assisted throughout by his brilliant draughtsman Augustus Pugin, who designed virtually all the decoration and details in metal, glass, tiles and wood. Barry's plan for the complex is clear and more Renaissance than Gothic: a spine of main chambers (the Royal Gallery, House of Lords, Lobbies, House of Commons) in line, with courts to either side and long ranges outside that. Pugin added an overlay of late perpendicular style detail, borrowed from the nearby Henry VII's Chapel, and such places as the church in Cirencester and the George Inn at Glastonbury.

At each end of the complex is a tower. The Victoria tower, 336 feet high, at the south end, sports a Union Jack during the daytime

The clock tower of Big Ben is London's most famous landmark. There is in fact no precedent for the ancient-looking design - it is a fairy tower with a top made up of pieces of pyramid. Like Tower Bridge, this extraordinary structure is now part of London's essential fabric.

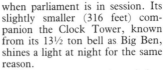

when parliament is in session. Its slightly smaller (316 feet) companion the Clock Tower, known from its 13½ ton bell as Big Ben, shines a light at night for the same reason.

The way government is carried on in the building has resulted in several curiosities. The monarch is not allowed into the House of Commons, but speaks from a throne in the House of Lords. In front of the throne is the Woolsack, seat of the Lord Chancellor, a cushion filled with wool, symbolising the importance of the wool trade to England in the 14th century.

The House of Commons was gutted by bombing in 1941, but in the years immediately after the War was rebuilt in very similar style. Even so, there are not enough seats for all 635 members of parliament.

The State Opening of Parliament takes place in late October or early November of each year. The monarch rides in the Irish State Coach to the Palace of Westminster, and enters the House of Lords amid much pomp and pageantry. The Commons are then summoned to the Lords for the ceremony itself.

179

TRACES OF EMPIRE

Traces of Britain's great mercan-
tile empire, and London's part in it,
can be found all over London.
Whereas the buildings of government were ornate, the buildings of
trade were often more simple,
functional and down-to-earth. This
is illustrated very well by the
complexes of warehouses which
have survived: Cutlers' Gardens
near Bishopsgate, now converted

*Above: one of the
refurbished ware-
house blocks at St
Katherine's Dock,
just downstream of the
Tower of London.
Right, Cleopatra's
Needle on the
Embankment.*

into plush office suites; and St Katherine's Dock.

The group of warehouses and basins that make up St Katherine's dock was designed by Thomas Telford, the great engineer, and finished in 1828. The warehouses were mostly for the storage of wine and wool. The dock closed in 1968, and since then has been imaginatively converted and restored into a complex of yachting marinas, a floating museum, flats, shops and offices. Look out for the elephants at the gates, and the Dickens public house, a timber-framed building from the former dock, which has sawdust on the floor.

Two further monuments to the Empire are worthy of note: Cleopatra's Needle on the Embankment, and the *Cutty Sark*, now permanently moored at Greenwich.

Cleopatra's Needle was presented to Britain by Mehemet Ali, a viceroy of Egypt, in 1819. It had an eventful sea journey from Egypt (described in a display at the Museum of London), and was erected in its present position in 1879. The Needle originally stood in Heliopolis, and was built to celebrate the

Sun – sad that it seems to have little effect on the London weather! It is one of a pair erected 3,500 years ago, long before Cleopatra's time. The other one now stands in Central Park, New York.

The *Cutty Sark* was built in 1869 and restored in a dry dock in 1957. Though now without her sails, she is a splendid reminder of the merchant ships (she was a tea clipper) which would have been seen in great numbers in the lower Thames up to the turn of the century.

She was launched at Dumbarton on the Clyde in Scotland. The name *Cutty Sark* is taken from the poem 'Tam O'Shanter' by Robert Burns, in which one of the witches at a coven dances in a cutty sark or short shirt. Officially opened as an exhibit in 1957, the ship contains material on its own history and a collection of ships' figureheads. She stands as a permanent reminder of the days when Britain dominated the world's oceans, exporting the products of the Industrial Revolution to the four corners of the globe, and bringing back exotic goods from the furthest reaches of the Empire to London's thriving docks.

Above: one of the exotic designs for the cast-iron seats on the Embankment; also to be found are camels. Right: the Cutty Sark *at her permanent berth at Greenwich. Nearby is another famous boat, Sir Francis Chichester's* Gispy Moth IV.

THE BATTLE OF THE STYLES

Victorian architecture is extremely varied in style, drawing as it did on nearly every previous fashion at some point or other. The Greek revival of the early 19th century disappeared in the 1840s (the colonnaded front of the British Museum is just about the last example). The Gothic revival (sometimes spelt 'Gothick') originated in the 18th century, and received official approval with the stipulations of the competition for the new Palace of Westminster in 1834. The Revival was at its strongest between 1840 and 1880, and London contains from this time the Law Courts in the Strand (1874-82) and St Pancras Station (1877).

At the same time an interest in the Italian High Renaissance, as seen in Florence and Rome, produced a competing Italianate style. The most important buildings in the early development of this fashion were the Travellers' Club (1829) and the Reform Club (1837), both by

St Pancras, one of the most exciting Victorian buildings in the world to look at. Though now converted to offices, the front was built as a

hotel. Imagine it when it was full of hundreds of guests and their servants, and surrounded by clouds of steam!

Charles Barry, next to each other in Pall Mall. Aristocratic clubs in the area of Piccadilly and St James had been popular since the 18th century. Based on the Italian palazzo, this style became very popular with medium-sized buildings throughout London. The inner courtyard at the Travellers' was open to the sky, as are its Florentine and Roman models, but at the Reform, Barry was persuaded to cover it with a glazed skylight in deference to the climate.

The Victorian age was also the era of prefabrication and architecture as engineering. Joseph Paxton's Crystal Palace, erected in Hyde Park for the Great Exhibition in 1851, was as large as the Houses of Parliament and yet took nine months to erect rather than 25 years. The structural system of cast-iron girders and glass sheets was quickly adapted for railway stations, as at King's Cross and Paddington (by Brunel). Paxton's friend W.H. Barlow designed the train shed at St Pancras, a massively simple structure (and for many years, the largest clear span in the world), in complete contrast to the hotel by Gilbert Scott (1868-77)

Detail of the facade of St Pancras station, giving a vivid illustration of medieval influences at work.

which forms the famous frontage.

The facade remained as a hotel until it was closed and turned into offices in 1935. Scott had made a study of French and Italian medieval details for a new government Foreign Office he hoped to build in Whitehall, but having been rejected for that he was able to pour them into this design. Touches of Venice mingle with memories of Westminster Abbey, Amiens and Salisbury Cathedrals. The skyline forms one of the most romantic silhouettes in London (especially against the setting sun).

The facades of the railway stations of London (most of which, like Paddington, were designed as large hotels) are a catalogue of the many styles in Victorian architecture. Pause then, before you hurry in for your train, and look at the outer front. At Charing Cross it is Venetian; at St Pancras a blend of European medieval; at Liverpool Street, Gothic (with 13th-century windows recalling the Bethlem Hospital of that date buried beneath the platforms), while Paddington is French Renaissance. The others are interesting within, not outside.

187

VICTORIAN ENGINEERING

Some idea of the achievements of Victorian engineering, and perhaps something of the spirit of Victorian shopkeeping, can still be gained by looking at four London market buildings: Covent Garden, Leadenhall, Smithfield and Billingsgate. Their fortunes also illustrate how varied the reactions of our own generation to these large buildings can be.

Covent Garden was originally a 17th-century square surrounded on three sides by town houses (see p. 128), but in 1670 the Duke of Bedford established a market in the square. Special buildings for the market, which had become predominantly for vegetables, were built in 1828-30 (the Market) and 1858-60 (the Floral Hall, to the north-east). The market, built by Charles Fowler, was restored by the Greater London Council in the 1970s. Situated at the centre of London's theatreland, it is now a popular and fashionable covered shopping precinct with performing musicians, jugglers, acrobats and other artistes. The structure itself forms two market halls with a central arcade; the exterior is of Tuscan columns with guard houses or lodges at the outer corners.

Three Victorian market buildings were erected in the City itself, on sites that had already been markets for generations: Smithfield for meat; Billingsgate for fish; and Leadenhall for food, especially poultry. They were all designed by the City architect, Sir Horace Jones.

Smithfield Market, on the site of a great open space where cattle had been sold since medieval times, was built in 1866-7. Its style is Italian, with octagonal domed corner towers. The four trading halls are based around Grand Avenue, East Poultry Avenue and West Poultry Avenue. Because the main hours of the market are in the very early morning, Smithfield always has a strange deserted air about it to the daytime visitor.

Jones then went on to replace the market building at Billingsgate in Thames Street, on the riverside (1875). This has an impressive pediment to the street, incorporating a large seated Britannia. Inside, until the market closed in

1981, the lofty hall resounded to the cries of fish sellers and porters with stacks of boxes on their heads. In the early morning the street outside was congested with porters' trolleys. Many small premises in the surrounding streets were small fish shops fed by the market; but it mainly acted as a distribution centre for lorries to take fish throughout Britain. The market hall has been preserved and is part of the development which includes the startling new blue glass building alongside.

Leadenhall Market was built in 1881. At present (1986), the Market is part of a wholesale rebuilding scheme incorporating much of the surrounding area. Formerly its frontage to Gracechurch Street was lost on the visitor, who only appreciated the great cross-shape of glass-roofed alleys. Today it is the nearest one can get in London to an oriental bazaar; the wares are still mostly poultry with some fish and fruit, and the whole precinct is thronged at lunch-times with many office workers buying their provisions. The Market still serves the population of the City, though they live elsewhere.

Leadenhall Market is a truly remarkable survival among the glass and concrete blocks of the modern City of London. Come in the lunch-hour for its best bazaar-like affect. Here you can get the best poultry and game in London and many other things, including pet food!

TOWER BRIDGE

The Port of London which largely supplied these markets lay along the City's waterfront, but especially between London Bridge (the 700-year-old medieval bridge was replaced in 1831-3) and a new bridge a short distance downstream – Tower Bridge. This was built in 1886-94 to the designs of John Wolfe Barry and Horace Jones. The two Gothic towers are steel skeletons clothed in stone. The upper bridge (now a viewing point and museum) was intended as a pedestrian walkway, while the lower bridge can be opened for large shipping. This was one of the original design stipulations, for the Pool of London between this bridge and London Bridge was then swarming with shipping. A passage 200 feet wide and 135 feet high had to be left for the tall ships to pass through. The bascules (those sections of the roadway which lift up) were electrified in 1976, but some of the original hydraulic machinery is preserved.

Tower Bridge does not appeal to everyone: the architectural authority Nikolaus Pevsner says 'the

Tower Bridge is attractive because it is unique - a Victorian invention. The towers originally housed the lifting machinery

which was powered by steam. The upper gallery is now open to give splendid views up and down the River Thames.

massive structure does much damage to the skyline of the City, and the apparent scale of the Tower of London' – but Tower Bridge remains for many visitors one of the supreme symbols of London's architecture.

193

VICTORIAN BUSINESS BUILDINGS

While in the City, among the glass and concrete skyscrapers of today, it is worth a quick walk around the streets of the ancient 'Square Mile' to capture sight of a few notable Victorian office buildings, now a precious rarity. They give some hint

Now dwarfed by the NatWest tower behind and facing a very unsuccessful 1980s concoction of a bank, the National Westminster Bank of 1863-5 is single-storeyed, proud, 'done with much swagger' as the architectural authority Nikolaus Pevsner says.

of the bustling capital of the Victorian empire – buildings in a variety of styles but all geared to the display and creation of wealth.

Near the Tower of London can be seen one of the most bizarre buildings in the City: 33-35 Eastcheap. This was designed as a vinegar warehouse and office building in 1868 by Robert Lewis Roumieu (1814-77), who worked on housing and minor public buildings in the London area. The sources for its weird window-forms and decoration is Venice (compare the arches of the Doge's Palace in St Mark's Square) and medieval gothic. It has been called variously 'as near to expressing evil as a design can be', 'utterly undisciplined and crazy' and 'the scream you wake on at the end of a nightmare'.

Not far away, in Bishopsgate, is the National Westminster Bank, built in 1863-5. Here a medium-sized bank tries to look like its parent, the Bank of England a few yards away. It employs tall Corinthian columns, and much sculpture. The frieze illustrates the arts, commerce, manufacture, science, agriculture and navigation. Above, figures represent the towns served by the Bank: London, Birmingham, Dover and Manchester. The last is represented by a female figure with a negro and raw cotton on one side, a workman with a bale of goods on the other.

At the heart of the City of London are the Bank of England and the Stock Exchange – although these no longer have their 19th-century appearances – and The Royal Exchange, by William Tite (1844), which is no longer used as a public building but has been converted into offices. At the southeast corner of the Exchange is a pump erected in 1799, bearing a depiction of the previous Royal Exchange which burned down in 1838.

MORE OF THE GOTHIC REVIVAL

Meanwhile the proliferation of architectural styles continued. It was only in large buildings that the taste for a Gothic Revival could be really indulged, and between the City and Westminster are two complexes which demonstrate this.

The Law Courts in the Strand were designed in 1866, and built in 1874-82. They adapt the style of greater English buildings in the 13th century. The skyline is a varied mixture of towers, corbelled turrets, gables, and a tall flèche (or slender spire) over the great hall. A monument to the architect, George Street, stands in the great hall; below Street, holding a pair of dividers, are depicted all the architectural skills, such as metal-working and stone-carving.

Nearby in Holborn is the Prudential Assurance building by Alfred Waterhouse (1879-1906). It somehow lacks the charm of the Law Courts or the craziness of St Pancras, but it dominates the hill as one comes out of the City over Holborn viaduct. The fiery red bricks and terracotta, perhaps a reaction to the polluted atmosphere of Victorian London, seem to sit easily across the road from the timber-framed frontage of Staple Inn, even though this, being a fictitious concoction, is just as irrelevant to the real ancient building as a modern glass-walled tower block would be.

WILLIAM MORRIS

One person who studied the medieval world in a different and much more accurate way was William Morris. He created new designs in the medieval fashion, but the details were based on a real knowledge of the period. The influence of Morris and his colleagues on the history of buildings and design is confined largely to decoration and furniture, though there is one notable house. Morris was a champion of the Arts and Crafts movement, learning and practising virtually all the skills of book printing and design, furniture making, wallpaper design and production, and other traditional crafts. His friends Webb and Burne-Jones produced interior designs, stained glass and tapestries.

Morris's first married home was built for him by Philip Webb: the Red House in Bexleyheath, then (1859) in the countryside. It is of red brick, with many steeply-pitched roofs, gables and dormer windows. 'More a poem than a house' said the pre-Raphaelite painter, Rossetti. Morris and his friends decorated the

William Morris was a prolific designer of wallpapers and fabrics in the 1870s and 1880s. This design for chintz was drawn from his deep love of nature as well as his familiarity with medieval illuminated manuscripts.

inside with wall-paintings and stained glass, and from this the firm of Morris & Co was born.

Stained glass by the company can be seen in several London churches. At Holy Trinity, Sloane Square, the Arts and Crafts movement is best displayed: ironwork, carving, and 48 small saints in stained glass by Edward Burne-Jones. In one window drawn by Rossetti, his sister Christina (the poet) appears as the Virgin, Jane Morris (William Morris' wife) as Mary Magdalene and Morris himself as Christ delivering the Sermon on the Mount. St Peter, Vere Street (Marylebone), St Luke, Caversham Road (Kentish Town), and All Saints, Lower Common (Wandsworth) are other churches with Morris & Co windows.

In 1867 the company was given its first large secular commission, the Green Dining Room in the new South Kensington Museum (now the Victoria and Albert Museum). Here, and in the furniture (such as the graceful William Morris chair) and wallpapers exhibited in the Museum, both his innovations and a certain naivety can be appreciated.

NORMAN SHAW

Norman Shaw (1831-1912) was one of the most influential late-19th-Century architects. Around 1870 he developed a style which combined Tudor half-timbering, Dutch Renaissance, Queen Anne, and ordinary house details from the 17th and 18th centuries, which he applied to country houses, office blocks and flats. A good example of his style is Swan House, Chelsea Embankment (1875), with late-17th-century projecting windows (possibly borrowed from Sparrow's House in Ipswich), with narrow 'Queen Anne' windows on the floor above.

In the 1880s Shaw and his circle moved further into Scottish baronial style, which incorporated features taken from continental baroque (French châteaux for example). The style is demonstrated by the Palace Theatre, Cambridge Circus (by Thomas Colcutt, 1890) – which, under its usual gigantic theatre hoarding, is actually quite alarming – and the imposing New Scotland Yard, Victoria Embankment, by Shaw (1888-90 and 1906). This two-part building, now called

Swan House, Chelsea Embankment: the doors, showing anticipation of the Art Nouveau style.

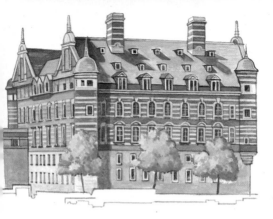

New Scotland Yard, by Shaw. Scottish baronial towers and striped brick and stone towards the base make a lively building. The skyline continues in procession along the Thames towards Blackfriars Bridge.

Norman Shaw Building North and South, since New Scotland Yard has moved to another, more modern building, is best seen from across the river. It shows a lively facade of brick and stone, which helped spread a revival in use of brick at this time – fortunately Shaw persuaded his clients not to have granite and Portland Stone as they wished. The pointed roofs on the corner turrets may have been intended to remind the viewer of the originally spiked helmets of London policemen.

Westminster
Cathedral is a
combination of Early
Christian and
Renaissance Italian
styles. Recent
clearance of the
buildings in front has
opened up a small
piazza, from which
the remarkable west
front can be
appreciated.

THE BYZANTINE STYLE: WESTMINSTER CATHEDRAL

Plans for a Roman Catholic cathedral in Westminster began in the 1860s, but an Early Christian (i.e. Byzantine) or Italian design was ordered, partly to avoid competition with the nearby Abbey. John Francis Bentley built Westminster Cathedral in 1897-1903. It is an unusual and successful combination of the two styles. The plan is a combination of Byzantine and Italian ideas, the dome an imitation of St Sophia in Istanbul; the tower (originally there were to be two) is similar to the campanile of Siena Cathedral, and is almost exactly the same height at 284 ft. The west portal is taken from the Italian Renaissance, and the red and white stripes of the walls are also Italian in inspiration (compare the cathedrals of Pisa and Padua). Inside, the intended decoration of marble and mosaics is only partially carried out, in fact helping to emphasise the vertical lines. Here also are the Stations of the Cross by Eric Gill, one of England's foremost 20th-century illustrators.

203

CURIOSITIES OF VICTORIAN LONDON

In central London there are many further curiosities of the Victorian age to look out for, some of them quite famous. One is the statue of Eros in Piccadilly Circus. This statue, by Alfred Gilbert, was erected in 1892 as a memorial to the benefactor Lord Shaftesbury. In fact it does not represent Eros (or Cupid) at all, but the Angel of Christian Charity, which referred to Shaftesbury's many good works.

There are also many odd little corners or peculiar bits of buildings, or things on the sides of buildings, which are relics of the Victorian age. The visitor should always pry into alleys and yards, always look around and up at the sides and backs of buildings. There may be a plaque on the wall, or a disused crane-arm, high up by a warehouse window above the shops; there may be little shops and workrooms virtually untouched by the 20th century. Public houses, theatres and even public conveniences may all on inspection yield a wealth of Victorian decoration and design.

The famous statue of Eros, recently refurbished as part of the redevlopment of Piccadilly Circus. The figure is not that of Eros, but of the Angel of Christian Charity.

These plaques in Postman's Park, Aldersgate, commemorate heroes in the early history of the Post Office.

THE LONDON UNDERGROUND

The first London Underground Railway ran from Paddington to Farringdon Street and was opened in January 1863. The trains were pulled by steam engines, and consisted of open trucks. Such was its novelty that within the first year it had carried nearly 9½ million passengers, equivalent to three times the population of London at that time. The Inner Circle Railway (now the Circle Line) was completed in 1884, the Piccadilly and Bakerloo Lines followed. Some of these underground stations still retain careful Victorian detailing, such as Art Nouveau ironwork and tiled booking offices. Many are being destroyed as old lifts or concourses are replaced, but the Circle Line platforms at Baker Street have recently been restored to something like their original state.

Smaller underground stations are often interesting examples of the varied ideas then current in Victorian architecture. A first-generation station of 1868, for instance, survives almost intact at Bayswater; nearby in Leinster Gardens are two dummy houses (nos. 23 and 24) to hide the lines below. The original type of station roof can be seen at Notting Hill and Paddington (Circle Line). The station at Gloucester Road has changed little since 1868.

Later Victorian stations show the influence of the Arts and Crafts movement: the timber station building at Earl's Court burned down in 1875 and was replaced with the present facade with balustrading and Arts and Crafts lettering. South Kensington is another example.

At first each route was a separate railway company, and traces of their

Covent Garden is one of the best examples of a station in the early 1900s. The ticket window is surrounded by green tiling; floral designs based on Arts and Crafts motifs

individual company badges or logos can be seen in many stations. The monogram of the London, Tilbury and Southend Railway can be seen in the canopy brackets at Bromley-by-Bow station; those of the Great Eastern Railway at Newbury Park. In the booking hall at Fulham Broadway is the symbol of the District Railway; the badge of the Metropolitan Railway is everywhere at Baker Street.

GROWTH OF THE SUBURBS

The coming of the industrial revolution and the rapid increase in London's population – from 959,000 in 1801 to 4½ million in 1901 – meant new systems of drainage and grand reclamation schemes such as the Thames Embankment. The suburban railway developed to promote and feed off the burgeoning suburbs. London's docklands expanded on a giant scale, requiring large areas of small artisan housing for the workers. Further out, housing estates for the middle class began to spread over hitherto green fields.

wind round the booking hall. Above the lifts are iron grilles with waving fronds. The station is also said to be the most haunted on the Underground!

207

TWENTIETH CENTURY LONDON

In the first decade of the 20th century, as befitted the capital of the world's largest empire, some monumental schemes of building were undertaken, among them Kingsway, the Mall, and Admiralty Arch.

In general, London's large buildings took on a rather graceless style – as in the east facade of Buckingham Palace (see p. 166), in such office buildings as the Port of London Authority headquarters, in Trinity Square by the Tower, and in numerous stores in Regent Street and Oxford Street (for example Selfridge's, begun 1908). The style tended to use grey stone and lots of monumental columns.

The largest of these constructions is Admiralty Arch (1910-11), through which the Mall is reached from Trafalgar Square. Together with the Memorial in front of Buckingham Palace, it formed part of the national memorial to Queen Victoria. It is now significant mainly as the starting point of a processional route for the sovereign to the Palace.

On the domestic front, London's population continued to increase, reaching 6½ million, the largest in the world. Suburban estates spread outwards from the city: one of them, Hampstead Garden Suburb (1906-15), was the first development to enshrine the concept of the Garden City, which had been put forward

Admiralty Arch (1906-11) is constructed of Portland stone, and is decorated with a Latin inscription, a tribute from Edward VII to his mother Queen Victoria. It completed a short ceremonial route to Buckingham Palace.

by various social reformers (particularly Ebenezer Howard). The scheme was to prove influential in much 20th-century city planning.

THE TWENTIES

The fabric of London was not greatly affected by the First World War, though there were a few Zeppelin air-raids. But the effect on the people was profound. Memorials to the hundreds of thousands who died in the trenches abound, and the annual Remembrance Day parade in Whitehall commemorates the Armistice of November 1918. After the War, London continued to grow in size. The last fields in the Greater London area were covered with housing. By 1931 the population of Greater London was 8.2 million, over twice the size it had been in 1871. In the inner ring of boroughs, the mostly densely occupied were Bethnal Green, Shoreditch, Southwark and Stepney; the City of London itself already had its modern character of large office blocks with very few people living within its boundaries. Further out,

The twenties saw the development of the transport system, enabling many thousands of workers to reach the City. St Paul's is a typical underground station at the time; notice the office girls, then a new phenomenon.

housing estates filled out the boroughs of West Ham, Bexley, Croydon, Sutton and Cheam, Ealing, Willesden, Finchley and Tottenham. Especially on the north side of the Thames, the underground railway was developed into a suburban network, encouraging many people to settle in the relative spaciousness of suburbia. The age of the city commuter had arrived.

211

ARCHITECTURAL STYLES

New ideas were introduced into the capital rather cautiously, but, from the 1920s onwards, the influence of continental styles – Art Deco, the Bauhaus – and of individual architects – Le Corbusier and Mies van der Rohe – began to be felt.

One of the most remarkable products of this was the Daily Express building in Fleet Street (1931), with its polished black or transparent glass and chromium strips. The corner is rounded, the facing smooth and uninterrupted except for the upper storeys which are set back; none of this was usual in 1931. The main designer, Sir Owen Williams, also built well-designed factories. The curtain-like wall, originally designed for factories, was later taken up by offices and large department stores (e.g. Peter Jones in Sloane Square (1936)).

The inside of the Daily Express foyer is, by contrast, all that is peculiar and dated about the 1930s; many colours in inlaid stone, a ceiling with light fittings vaguely reminiscent of a late medieval vault,

Owen Williams' Daily Express *building (1932) represents an original and enigmatic approach which sadly did not go any further. The same architect was never again so daring or innovative in his designs.*

and metal relief wall sculptures depicting colonial enterprises. The staircase is in the spirit of the entrance to Cleopatra's tomb, complete with snakes as handrails. This is called the Art Deco style. A more harmonious example of the style is a block of two of Selfridge's lifts, built in 1928 for the Oxford Street store, and now in the Modern Gallery of the Museum of London.

More monumental styling of the 1930s is seen at Broadcasting House, the headquarters of the BBC in Portland Place. The enormous facade has on it a sculptured group by Eric Gill, representing Prospero and Ariel.

LONDON IN THE BLITZ

It is difficult now to imagine London during the Second World War, or to see today the direct effects of the Blitz, the German bombing campaign of 1940-1. In the City, the indirect effects are very visible: office blocks of the 1950s and especially 1960s show where the bombs fell. Whole areas were obliterated, especially on the night

Designs from the lift at Selfridge's store; below the lift itself is in the Modern Gallery of the Museum of London.

of 29 December, 1940: in one raid large parts of the western part of the City were destroyed – the area north of St Paul's Cathedral, now the Paternoster Square development, and the Barbican area further north. Indeed, but for worsening weather which made flying impossible, there would have been a second raid the same night which would certainly have destroyed St Paul's and the rest of the City.

There are few remaining traces of the War to be seen in London streets. In the City, two churches remain as open ruins (St Dunstan in the East, and Christchurch Newgate Street). Aldersgate Undergound Station, renamed Barbican, still shows the supports of its original roof before the bombing. In the West End, The Windmill Theatre, earned its slogan-'We never close' by operating throughout the Blitz.

There are, however, many reminders of the war at the Imperial War Museum south of the river. And on the river itself, at Symon's Wharf, is HMS *Belfast*, the last of the Royal Navy's big-gun cruisers, and now a floating museum of naval actions during World War II.

HMS Belfast *now a floating museum at permanent anchor in the Pool of London. She escorted Arctic convoys to Russia and took part in the D-Day landings in 1944.*

THE SOUTH BANK

After the hardships of war and the
rigours of postwar austerity, the
country needed a symbol of rejuven-
ation and hope for the future. It was
provided by the South Bank complex, the first part of which, the
Royal Festival Hall, was completed
in time for the Festival of Britain in

1951. The remainder of the complex
– the Hayward Gallery, the Queen
Elizabeth Hall, the National Film
Theatre, and the National Theatre –
came later, as did the nearby Shell
Building.

The Royal Festival Hall,
designed by Robert Matthew and
Leslie Martin, is of more interest
internally than externally. This is
partly because of the varied materials and textures - lots of glass,
with wooden surfaces, grey Derby-
shire marble slabs, and textiles - but
also because of the intricate ups and
downs of staircases, landings and
galleries. The Hayward was built for
art exhibitions and so this too really
works only on the inside, as a series

The Royal Festival Hall, opened in 1951. Inside, the hall has boxes like a theatre, but placed so oddly that a critic called them 'like drawers pulled out in a hurried burglary raid'. The building continues to be a great success as a concert hall.

of rooms of different sizes to be exploited by exhibitions. The National Theatre (1961-76), by Sir Denys Lasdun, was the last of the buildings to be completed. The main material is concrete, complete with the marks left by the shuttering into which it was poured. The skyline is dominated by functional towers - fly towers, which hold the scenery high above the National's three stages.

The South Bank sums up much of the public architecture of the sixties and seventies. The style is sometimes called Brutalism: deliberate lack of symmetry, concentration on large hunks of building, use of concrete. At the same time, the intricate system of interconnecting stairs and walkways, the unexpected changes of level and direction, and the varied rooflines and views of the river, provide a constantly interesting kaleidoscope of new sights.

THE BARBICAN

Another post-war development, this time near the heart of the City, is the Barbican. Here, 60 acres of

217

bomb-blasted London, mostly housing, had to be rebuilt, and the opportunity was taken to plan blocks of flats, schools, a museum (the Museum of London), office blocks and an Arts Centre. The restored St Giles Cripplegate church, where John Milton is buried, now lies beside playing fountains and, weather permitting, a sunny continental promenade with cafe and outside tables.

Critics have attacked the mixture of post-War styles in the architec-

The Barbican: view of the main concert hall and theatre complex, across a lake with playing fountains. Despite yellow lines on the ground which lead the visitor into the labyrinth, many people still get lost among the high buildings.

ture (the result of a building programme lasting 30 years), the windy emptiness and the complete severance from the rest of the City. They also, with some justice, complain of the maze of walkways which, as in some ancient labyrinth, seem to lead the visitor ever further from his or her destination. Nevertheless, the Barbican flourishes as a national arts centre, and City workers have come to appreciate the cinemas, theatres and art galleries offered in the central complex.

THE CHANGING SKYLINE

The London Telecom or Post Office Tower in Warren Street was built in 1963-6. At 174m (580ft) high it was the tallest building in London until the erection of the NatWest Tower in 1981. It marked the start of the trend to high-rise office (and residential) building which, while not of Manhatten-like proportions, was to change once and for all the skyline of London.

Unfortunately, many of the medium-sized towers especially in the City, are of a boring pink granite and glass combination with all the simplicity of wooden building-blocks. Other examples are more dramatic. Centre Point at the junction of Tottenham Court Road and New Oxford Street, was notorious for being left empty for several years as office rents escalated. The pavements around the building hardly hold the bustling tourists and workers, who have to negotiate the fountains or pass under the buildings great feet.

The National Westminster Bank (NatWest) Tower in Old Broad Street in the City, was finished in 1981. It is 600 ft (183m) high, and is Britain's tallest building. It was built by the same architects as Centre Point, the Richard Seifert partnership. It dominates any view of the city from the south.

There are signs that completely new architectural styles and techniques are emerging. A new approach can be seen in Richard Rogers' new Lloyds building in Leadenhall Street, EC3 (opened in 1987). The building is totally inward looking - stunning from the inside, but putting all its services – pipes, heating ducts and so on – on

Rising over the Charlotte Street restaurant quarter, the Post Office Tower seemed in the 1960s to be a symbol of the future. Now its revolving restaurant is closed, and it has become another accepted feature of the modern skyline.

the outside. A concern with *internal* space, inherited from the Pompidou Centre in Paris (1977) by the same architect, has taken over from external statements of wealth or power.

There are certain hopeful signs for London's heritage in the future. Because of the high cost of construction, many smaller and medium-sized old buildings are being refurbished instead of being knocked down. A city needs buildings of many sizes – large and small – and older buildings can be adapted to many useful purposes without radical alteration. At the same time an increasing concern with the environment has led to the establishment of many small public gardens and care for open spaces.

We can always learn from study of the past. We can see how London grew from its Roman origins, through many changes, to achieve its present form. And in so doing we shall be able to appreciate the historical events and personalities that have shaped the fabric and character of England's capital. And we shall, perhaps, be able to plan better for the future.

221

LONDON'S MUSEUMS

The following is a selected list of some of London's most important or more interesting museums, with the emphasis on those that specifically illustrate some aspect of the city's history. Although the main listing is in alphabetical order, we must start with:

The **Museum of London**, London Wall, EC2 (open Tues-Sat, Sun p.m.). Here will be found much exciting and interesting material to illustrate all the themes in this book. The Museum, a result of the fusion of the London Museum and the Guildhall Museum in 1975, is dedicated to the archaeology and history of London and its people. The main galleries are arranged in chronological order, from prehistory to the modern age. Throughout the displays there are reconstructions of period rooms - a Roman house in London, a medieval kitchen, a 17th-century panelled room (with period music), Victorian and early modern shops (a barber's, a bank, a chemist's, and even Woolworth's). The visitor can experience the Great Fire or listen to the wailing of the air-raid sirens in the Blitz; shiver in a cell from Newgate jail; and inspect the Lord Mayor's Coach. There is also a continuous programme of talks and workshops by Museum staff to illustrate the collections and what they tell us about different aspects of London's history.

All Hallows by the Tower, Byward Street, EC3, (Mon-Sat) has a collection of material excavated on the site, from part of a Roman house to early modern clay pipes; the church has the City's only fragment of Saxon work.

Apsley House (Wellington Museum), 14a Piccadilly, W1, (Tues, Thurs, Sat, Sun p.m.) was originally built by Adam but enlarged in 1828 as a residence for the Duke of Wellington. Together with memorabilia of the Duke are trophies from the grateful nation, including an 11-foot statue of a near-naked Napoleon.

At the **Bear Gardens Museum**, Bear Gardens, SE1, (daily) is an exhibition concerning the Elizabethan theatre. The Museum stands on the site of the last bear-baiting ring on Bankside, and is close to the site of Shakespeare's Globe Theatre.

The **Bethnal Green Museum of Childhood**, Cambridge Heath Road, E2, (Mon-Thurs, Sat, Sun p.m.) is devoted to toys, dolls' houses and model soldiers – recommended for children of all ages. The building was originally a gallery at the South Kensington (V&A) Museum, built of cast iron, and was moved to Bethnal Green in 1875 in an attempt to bring art to the working people. What should a museum for the working classes look like? This one has overtones of a railway station.

The **British Museum**, Great Russell Street, WC1, (Mon-Sat, Sun p.m.) has already figured in our story (p. 174). When you have finished admiring Smirke's portico with its great columns, go inside – if only for a taste! Like all major museums and galleries, the British Museum is best seen over many visits. Some parts are always seen first, like the Elgin Marbles or the Egyptian Galleries. For the history of London, see the Roman Gallery (with much London material in it), and the Saxon and medieval displays (for instance the beautiful room of medieval tiles).

Carlyle's House, 24, Cheyne Row, SW3, (Wed-Sat, Sun p.m.) houses some memorabilia of Thomas Carlyle, and the interior gives a good impression of a 19th-century writer's house; see also the garden.

Chiswick House, Burlington Lane, Chiswick, W4, (summer, daily; winter Wed-Sun) is described on p. 154. This famous 18th-century house has a beautiful setting.

The **Court Dress Collection**, Kensington Palace, W8, (Mon-Sat. Sun p.m.) is a collection of royal and aristocratic dresses.

Cuming Museum, 155-7 Walworth Road, SE17, (Mon-Fri) is devoted primarily to the history of Southwark (the district of London which lay over London Bridge to the south of the City), but also has a collection relating to superstitions in London.

Cutty Sark, Greenwich Pier, SE10, (Mon-Sat, Sun p.m.) has been preserved in dry dock at Greenwich since 1957. Visiting this ship is a natural climax to a day investigating London's nautical heritage – combine it with the National Maritime Museum in Greenwich, and if possible, arrive by boat down the Thames from Tower Pier.

The **Dickens House Museum**, Doughty Street, WC1, (Mon-Sat) holds memorabilia of Charles Dickens, one of the great commentators on London life in the 19th century, and himself largely a product of the metropolis. Here he worked on *Pickwick Papers*, *Oliver Twist*, *Nicholas Nickelby* and other books; here the young writer created Fagin and the Artful Dodger.

The **Epping Forest Museum**, Queen Elizabeth's Hunting Lodge, Rangers Road, Chingford, E4, (Wed-Sun p.m.) is housed in a Tudor hunting lodge, one of London's very few remaining timber-framed buildings. The royal parties would have observed the chase from the upper floor; note that there was no glass in the windows, even for royalty. In Tudor times, Chingford was largely forest; today, some imagination is required to place the building and its exhibits (the story of Epping Forest and local archaeology) in context.

The **Museum of Garden History** (Mon-Fri) is to be found in the former church of St Mary at Lambeth, Lambeth Palace Road, SE1. It contains the history of the gardening Tradescant brothers, and general gardening history.

The **Geffrye Museum**, Kingsland Road, Shoreditch, E2, (Mon-Sat, Sun p.m.) is a series of period rooms illustrating social history since 1606. The building is the former almshouses of the Ironmongers' Company (the modern descendant of the medieval guild). The almshouses were built in 1715 beyond the end of the houses then in Shoreditch, i.e. facing the countryside; lime trees were planted in front in 1719. In these peaceful surroundings the older members of the company or their widows could spend their retirement. Almshouses of the other livery companies can be found in several other London boroughs; their locations usually show where pleasant suburbia in the countryside was to be found when they were built.

The **Guildhall Clock Museum** (Mon-Fri) is found in the Guildhall complex in Aldermanbury, EC2. The collection contains over 700 clocks, watches and chronometers belonging to the Clockmaker's Company.

HMS Belfast (daily) lies at anchor at Symonds Wharf, Vine Lane, SE1. Now a floating museum, she was built in 1939, and is the largest cruiser ever built for the Royal Navy.

Hogarth's House, Hogarth Lane, Chiswick, (Mon-Sat, Sun p.m.) contains Hogarth personalia, drawings and watercolours. Close by, in the churchyard of St Nicholas, is a monument to the artist; Lord Burlington and his protegé William Kent are buried here.

In the **Horniman Museum**, London Road, Forest Hill, SE23, (Mon-Sat, Sun p.m.) is a collection of musical instruments from all over the world, and other exhibits. It is a remarkable building: designed to house the collections of an M.P., F.J. Horniman, in 1897-1901. It shows influences of the Byzantine and Arts and Craft movements (compare Westminster Cathedral of the same period) and perhaps American building ideas. In the gardens is a sculptured group of figures and a pelican of 1797, made of Coade stone, the artificial 'stone' whose formula is now lost. The group came originally from a building in Lombard Street.

The Imperial War Museum, Lambeth Road, SE1, (daily) concentrates on the military history of Britain and the Commonwealth from 1914 to the present.

The Iveagh Bequest, Kenwood, Hampstead Lane, NW3, (daily) better known as Kenwood, is a magnificent 18th-century mansion in beautiful grounds, bequeathed to the nation in 1928. The paintings include many old masters, but look out for the view of Old London Bridge about 1640 by de Jongh, a long narrow painting. Notice how the Tower of London has moved its site – it is seen dimly in its correct position, in the distance through an arch of the bridge, but also much more prominently in the wrong place near the foreground! But otherwise the painting is a valuable source of information about the riverfronts of the City and Southwark before the Great Fire of 1666.

Dr Johnson's House, Gough Square, EC4, (Mon-Sat) holds memorabilia of the great 18th-century writer and compiler of Johnson's Dictionary. It was Johnson who remarked that 'a man who is tired of London is tired of life'.

Keats' House, Wentworth Place, Keats Grove, Hampstead, NW3, (Mon-Sat, Sun p.m.) holds some personal belongings of the poet John Keats. He only lived in one half of it· when it was two houses; it was unified after his death. Very plain, but gives a good idea of a small house in the Regency period. 19th-century artists would still feel at home in the surrounding streets.

Kew Bridge Engines Trust and Water Supply Museum, Green Dragon Lane, Brentford, Middlesex, (daily; engines in steam weekends and Bank Holidays) is for those interested in stationary steam engines and water pumping equipment.

The London Dungeon, 28-34 Tooley Street, SE1, (daily) is a horrifying experience, with scenes of torture and murder in dark, dingy vaults beneath a railway viaduct. A little overdone, but children love it!

The **London Transport Museum**, Covent Garden, WC2, (daily) concentrates on the history of London Transport, and has a fine collection of buses, trains and trams.

In the **Maritime Trusts Museum, Historic Ships Collection**, St Katherine Dock, E1, (daily) can be found a number of British sailing and steam-powered vessels of the 19th and early 20th centuries, including a lightship. Here may be moored some of the small sailing craft which used to transport goods and people up and down the Thames.

The **National Gallery**, Trafalgar Square, W1, (Mon-Sat, Sun p.m.) is a familiar building on the north side of the Square. If you stand back far enough to appreciate the whole facade, you will realise that the frontage is composed of no less than 13 sections, all of approximately the same width and emphasis, so that the central portico and dome is not very dominant. Inside, the Gallery's 46 rooms cover the history of European painting from the 13th century to the early 20th. As with all national art galleries, it takes several visits to appreciate them.

The **National Maritime Museum**, Romney Road, Greenwich, SE10, (Mon-Sat, Sun p.m.) has a spectacular collection of boats, models, seascapes, and objects associated with great naval heroes or explorers such as Nelson (including the uniform he wore at the Battle of Trafalgar) and Captain Cook. The Museum shows the development of Britain as a seafaring nation.

The **National Portrait Gallery** (Mon-Sat, Sun p.m.) is next to the National Gallery, in Charing Cross Road, WC2. Here the visitor can absorb more pictures in each visit. Besides the portraits of royalty from earliest times to the present Royal Family, there are many portraits of persons associated with London (e.g. in the history of broadcasting and the cinema).

Passmore Edwards Museum, Romford Road, Stratford, E15, (Mon-Fri) is the museum for the London boroughs east of the river Lea (i.e. most of north-east London). It reflects the Essex connections with London; and runs an archaeological team to deal with the special problems of redevelopment in these outer parts, e.g. gravel quarrying. The Museum also has *Dawn*, an original Thames sailing barge; and North Woolwich Old Station, Pier Road, Woolwich E16, a restored Victorian station.

The **Museum of the Order of St John**, St John's Gate, St John's Lane, Clerkenwell, EC1, (Tues, Fri, Sat) displays the history of the Order of St John of Jerusalem, in London's finest surviving monastic relic – the early 16th century north gate to the otherwise almost totally disappeared medieval priory.

The **Public Records Office Museum**, Chancery Lane, WC2, (Mon-Fri p.m.) displays many historic documents, including a copy of the *Domesday Book*. The name Chancery Lane is probably derived from the Chancellor of the Exchequer, an important royal official who settled his office in this 'New Street' in the 13th century. Among his many duties was the keeping of royal records.

At the **Ranger's House**, Chesterfield Walk, Blackheath, SE10, (daily) a collection of Jacobean and Stuart portraits is housed in one of a group of late 17th century houses built on the edge of Greenwich Park. It was refronted in the early 18th century, and the gallery housing the portraits was added in 1749-50.

Sir John Soane's Museum, 13 Lincoln's Inn Fields, WC2, (Tues-Sat) is a 19th-century private house, the studio of the architect Sir John Soane. It is curious, full of small intricately-decorated rooms, and cleverly confusing. Its Monk's Yard contains some medieval fragments from the palace of Westminster, assembled to form the tomb and cloister of a fictitious Padre Giovanni. It illustrates well the 18th- and 19th- century craze for collecting.

St Bride's Crypt Museum, St Bride's Church, Fleet Street, EC4, (daily) shows the various remains of the church's long history, including a fragment of a Roman building outside the Roman city walls.

The **Tate Gallery**, Millbank, SW1, (Mon-Sat, Sun p.m.) is on the site of the Millbank Penitentiary, a model prison of 1812-21; the octagonal shape of the prison is still evident in the street-pattern surrounding the Gallery, which was built in stages between 1897 and 1979. It houses the national collection of British works from the 16th century to the present, and is especially noted for its fine collection of modern art. One London painting to look out for is John Constable's *View of Hampstead*, painted in 1836, showing the open countryside and windmills in the years before London spread over the hills and rural villages to its north.

Tower Bridge, SE1, (daily) contains a display on the history of the bridge, and provides splendid views of the river and the City.

Upminster Tithe Barn, Hall Lane, Upminster, Essex, (1st weekend of month, April-Oct) is an important relic of rural building when London's suburbs were only fields; it dates from about 1450, and contains a display of agricultural equipment. Nearby in St Mary's Lane is the **Upminster Windmill** (open some weekend afternoons), complete with the original machinery.

The **Victoria and Albert Museum**, Cromwell Road, SW7, (Mon-Thurs, Sat, Sun p.m.) was promoted by Prince Albert to improve British design and technique in the arts, when Britain's supremacy and Empire was beginning to wane. It is now much more, having assembled an unrivalled collection of artistic objects from all over the world. For London's history, see the woodwork gallery, with 16th- to 19th-century facades, doorcases, and especially the house-front of Sir Paul Pindar's house from Bishopsgate (1597), removed to make way for Liverpool Street Station; and the medieval and early modern furnishings, including medieval chests and cupboards, tapestries, hangings and cushions, and displays concerning William Morris and his circle.

In the **Wallace Collection**, Hertford House, Manchester Square, W1, (Mon-Sat, Sun p.m.) can be found armour, porcelain, clocks, miniatures and many old master paintings, including the *Laughing Cavalier* by Frans Hals. The collection is displayed in an 18th-century town house.

Walthamstow Museum, Old Vestry House, Vestry Road, Walthamstow, E17, (Mon-Fri) is located in a workhouse built in 1730; the surrounding buildings, including a Tudor cottage and 18th-century almshouses, show something of the suburban, almost rural village in which William Morris grew up. The Museum illustrates local history. Nearby, at Lloyd Park, Forest Road, Walthamstow is the house where Morris spent much of his childhood, now the the home of the **William Morris Gallery** (Mon-Sat, 1st Sun in month). Many of his designs and artefacts are here.

The **Whitechapel Art Gallery**, Whitechapel High Street, E1, (Mon-Fri, Sun) was, like the Bethnal Green Museum, a contribution to the cultural life of the East End. It encourages local artists and has important exhibitions of contemporary art. The striking building of 1897-9 was designed by Harrison Townsend, who also designed the Horniman Museum. It is a rare example of Art Nouveau style applied to a building in London.

INDEX

*London's Museums are not included in the index but are listed in alphabetical order on pp. 222-34. References in **bold** type are to illustrations.*

Adam, Robert, 157, 159
Admiralty Arch, 165, **208**, 209
Admiralty Screen, 157
Albert, Prince, 171-2
Albert Hall, 172-3, **173**
Albert Memorial, 171-2, **172**
Alfred, king, 29-32
All Hallows Barking, 21, 27, **28**, 37, 90
All Saints, Wandsworth, 199
Anne, Queen, 68
Anne of Bohemia, 101
Apsley House, 161
Arts and Crafts Movement, 198, 206
Art Deco, 212-3
Art Nouveau, 206
Augustine, St, 25

Banqueting House,
    Whitehall, 125-6, **126**,
    130, 137-8, 155
Barbican, 217-9, **218**
Barlow, W.H., 186
Barry, Charles, 178, 184
Barry, John Wolfe, 192
Bayeux Tapestry, 38, **40**
Beefeaters, 53, **53**
Bede, 27

Bedford Row, 158
Big Ben, Westminster, **179**, 179
Billingsgate, 188-9
Blackfriars, **69**, 69-71
Blitz, the, 83, 213-4
Boadicea, see Boudica
Boar's Head, Eastcheap, **149**
Boleyn, Anne, 52
Boudica **10**, 11
British Museum, **174**, 174-6
Broadcasting House, 213
Brunel, Isambard, 186
Buckingham, Duke of, 166
Buckingham Palace, **166**,
    166-9, 209
Burlington, Lord, 154
Burton, Decimus, 161

Campbell, Colin, 154
Canterbury, 29
Canute, king, see Cnut
Centre Point, 220
Chambers, William, 157
Changing the Guard, **168**, 169
Charles I, king, 127
Charles II, king, 148
Chelsea Pensioners, 147
Cheyne Row, 158
Chiswick House, **154**, 154
Christ Church, Spitalfields,
    150, **150**
Christchurch Newgate St, 214
Churches; Saxon, see All
    Hallows Barking, St Bride
    Fleet St; medieval, 90-3;
    by Wren, **140-1**, 141-2
Churchill, Winston, 108

City Companies, 84-5
City of London, arms, **78**, 78
City wall, Roman, **18**, 18-9,
19, **22**, **23**; 48; medieval,
69-71, **70**
Clarence, Duke of, 54
Cleopatra's Needle, **181**, 181
Cnut, king, 35-7
Constitution Arch, **160**, 161
Cordwainers, 84
Cornhill, 10, 13
Cosmati, 100
Covent Garden, 127-8,
188-9, **188**
Covent Garden Underground
station, **206**
Cripplegate fort, 15-7, **16**, **17**
Crosby, John, 86-7, 93
Crosby Place, **86**, 86-7, **87**
Crystal Palace, 172
Cumberland Terrace, **162**,
163
Cutlers' Gardens,
Bishopsgate, 180
Cutty Sark, 181, 182, **183**

Daily Express building, **212**,
212-3
Dance, George (the elder), 153
Dark Ages, 24-8
Dark earth, 24-5, **25**
Dickens Pub, 181
Docks, London, 180-2
Dudley, Guildford, 57
Duke of York's Watergate,
128

Edward the Confessor, 38, 94,
99
Edward I, king, 50
Edward III, king, 100
Edward IV, king, 54
Edward V, king, 54, 55, **107**
Edward VI, 56
Eleanor of Castile, 100-1
Elgin marbles, 174
Elizabeth I, queen, 93, 107
Elizabeth II, Queen, 168
Eltham Palace, 87-8, **89**
Ely Place, **72**, 74, 76
Eros, 204, **204**
Ethelbert, king, 25
Ethelred, king, 33

Forum, 14-15

George I, king, 154
George IV, statue, 165, 171
George Inn, 121
Gibbs, James, 150-2
Gill, Eric, 203, 213
Gladstone, William, 108
Goldsmiths, 84
Great Fire of 1666, 83, **132**,
132-4, 158
Grey, Lady Jane, 56-7, **57**
Greyfriars, 71
Guildhall, 80, 82-3, **82**, 134
Guilds, see City Companies
Guy Fawkes, **109**

Hampstead Garden Suburb, 209
Hampton Court, 112, 114-6, **115-6**, 146, **146**
Hastings, Battle of, 38-40
Hawksmoor, Nicholas, 145, 150, 176
Hayward Gallery, 216-7
Henry III, king, 50, 99, 100
Henry V, king, 80
Henry VI, king, 54
Henry VII, king, 112
Henry VIII, king, 52, 53, 93, 112, 114
HMS Belfast, **214**, 214
Hogarth, William, 155
Holy Trinity, Sloane Square, 199
Horse Guards' Parade, 155, 168
Houses, Saxon, 30-1; medieval, 72-6, 84, 86-7; Tudor, 119; 17th-century, 129-30; 18th-century, 148; Georgian, 158-63;
Houses of Parliament, 176-9, **177**
Howard, Catherine, 52
Hyde Park, 160-1
Hyde Park Corner, 161

Inns of Court, 116-8

John, king, 49, 80
Johnson, Samuel, 140

Johnson's house, 148, **149**
Jones, Horace, 189-92
Jones, Inigo, 112, 124-9, 137
Jonson, Ben, 108
Judd, Andrew, 93
Keats, John, 108
Kent, William, 154-5, 159
Kew Palace, 130, **131**
Keys, Ceremony of, 54
King's Cross Station, 186-7
Kitchener, Lord, 140

Lambeth Palace, 76
Lasdun, Denys, 217
Law Courts, **196**, 197
Leadenhall Market, 190, **190**
Lincoln's Inn, **117**, 117
Lincoln's Inn Fields, 129
Lindsey House, **129**, 129
Liverpool Street Station, 187
Lloyds building, 220-1
London; Roman, 10-23, **12**, **13**, **22**; Saxon, 24-41, **26**, **39**; medieval, 42-93, **64**; Tudor and Stuart, 112-49, **120**; Georgian, 150-63; Victorian, 164-207; 20th-century, 208-21; seal of, **66**;
London Bridge, Roman, 12, 32; Saxon, 32-3, **34**, 67; medieval, 66-7, **67**
London Bridge Station, 187
London Wall Walk, 19
Lord Mayor, 79-81, 152
Lord Mayor's Coach, 80, **80**

Lundenwic, see London,
    Saxon
Lutyens, Edwin, 165

Mansion House, 152-3, **153**
Marble Arch, 165, 170-1, **170**
    Martin, Leslie, 216
Mary, queen, 57
Matthew, Robert, 216
Merchant Taylors, 84; Hall,
    85
Middle Temple, 118, **118**
Milton, John, 108, 218
Monument, The, 134, **135**,
    142
More, Thomas, 52
Morris, William, **198**, 198-9
Museum of London, 15

Nash, John, 162-4, 166
National Gallery, 164-5
National Theatre, 217
National Westminster Bank,
    Bishopsgate, **194**, 195-6
Natural History Museum, 173
NatWest Tower, 220
Naval Hospital, Greenwich,
    143-4, 144-6
Nelson, Lord, 140
Nelson's Column, 164-5, **164**
New Scotland Yard, 201, **201**
Newgate, Roman, **19**

Olaf, king, 33

Paddington Station, 186-7
Pagoda, Kew, **157**
Palladian revival, 154-7
Paris, Louvre, 51, 146; Place
    des Vosges, 128;
    Pompidou Centre, 221;
    royal palace, 76
Parliament, Houses of,
    176-9; State Opening of,
    179
Paxton, Joseph, 186
Pepys, Samuel, 133
Peter Jones' store, 212
Piccadilly Circus, 204
Pickering, William, 93
Port of London Authority,
    209
Portman Square, **159**
Post Office (British Telecom)
    Tower, **219**, 219
Prince Henry's room, Fleet
    St, 120
Prince Regent (William IV),
    162, 166
Prudential Assurance
    Building, 197
Pugin, Augustus, 172, 178

Queen's House, Greenwich,
    123-4, 124-5, 145

Railway stations, 184-7
Reform Club, 184-5
Regent's Park, 163, **163**
Reynolds, Joshua, 140

Richard I, king, 49
Richard II, king, 101
Richard III, king, 55
Richard of York, 55, 107
Rochester, Robert, 93
Rotten Row, 161
Roumieu, Robert Lewis, 195
Royal Academy, Piccadilly, 154
Royal Artillery Corps monument, 161
Royal Exchange, 119, 196
Royal Festival Hall, 215-6, **216**
Royal Mews, 167
Royal Military Hospial, Chelsea, 146-7
Royal School of Music, 173

Saddlers, 84
St Andrew Undershaft, 90
St Bartholomew Smithfield, 58, **59, 61**
St Bride Fleet St, 21, 27
St Dunstan in the East, 214
St Ethelburga, 90
St Etheldreda, **75**
St George Bloomsbury, 176
St Giles Cripplegate, 218
St Helen Bishopsgate, 90-3, **92**
St James's Palace, **114**, 114
St Katherine's Dock, **180**, 181
St Lawrence Jewry, 142
St Magnus the Martyr, 142
St Martin Outwich, 93

St Martin-in-the-Fields, 151-2, **152**, 165
St Mary Woolnoth, 150, **151**
St Mary-le-Bow, **91**, 142
St Mary-le-Strand, 151, **152**
St Olave Hart St, 90
St Pancras Station, **184**, 184, 186-7
St Paul Covent Garden, 128
St Paul's, Saxon, 24-5, 38; **136-8**; medieval, **68**, 68-9, 134; by Wren, 137-41, **136-8**
St Paul's churchyard, 37
St Peter, Vere St, 199
St Peter Cornhill, 142
St Peter in the Tower, 52
Science Museum, 173
Scott, Gilbert, 171
Selfridge's lift, **213**
Selfridge's store, 209, 213
Serpentine, 161
Shakespeare, William, 93, 108, 121
Shaw, Norman, 200-1
Shelley, Parcy Bysshe, 108
Skinners, 84
Smirke, Robert, 175
Smirke, Sydney, 176
Smithfield Market, 188-9
Somerset House, 119, **156**, 157
South Bank, 215-7
Speakers' Corner, **161**, 161, 171
Staple Inn, 119, **122**
Strand settlement, 27

239

Street, George, 197
Swan House, Chelsea, 200, **200**
Swein of Denmark, 33

Telford, Thomas, 181
Temple, 61, **61**, **62**
Temple Bar, **147**
Temple Gardens, 29
Temple of Mithras, **20**, 21
Thames, River, 10
Thorkel the Tall, 33
Tower Bridge, **192**, 192-3
Tower Green, 53, 57
Tower Hill, 52, 57
Tower of London, **42**, 42-57, **45**, **48**; as a prison, 51-7; St John's Chapel, 44-7, **47**; Salt Tower, **55**; Traitors' Gate, 51; White Tower, 42-8, **44**
Trafalgar Square, 164-5, **165**
Traitors' Gate, 51
Travellers' Club, 184-5
Trooping the Colour, 168

Underground, 205-7, 211

Valence, Aymer de, 101
Valance, William de, 101
Victoria, queen, 53, 167, 171
Victoria & Albert Museum, 173, 199
Victoria Memorial, 167
Victoria Station, 187

Victoria Tower, Westminster, 178-9
Vikings, 29-37

Walbrook stream, **22**
Waterhouse, Alfred, 197
Wellington, Duke of, 140, 161
Westminster, 38, **39**, 64, 72
Westminster Abbey, 38, 63, 64, 94-111, **95-111**; chapter house, 102, **102-3**; church, 95-101; Dean's House, **104**, 105, **106**; Henry VII's chapel, 112-3, **113**; Innocents' Corner, 107, **108**; Poets' Corner, 107-8; royal burials, 99-101
Westminster Cathedral, **202**, 203
Westminster Hall, 109, **110-1**
Westminster Palace, 76, 109, **110-1**, 178
Whitefriars, 71
Whittington, Dick, **79**, 79-80
William the Conqueror, 39-44, 167
Williams, Owen, 212
Winchester Palace, 74, **74**
Windmill Theatre, 214
Wolsey, Cardinal, 140
Wordsworth, William, 108
Wren, Christopher, 129, 137-47

Yeomen of the Tower, 53
York, Jorvik Centre, 31